To

MARION
MARY and **ANN**

and

BILL

DATE DUE

MANAGEMENT:

Ends and Means

CHANDLER PUBLICATIONS IN
MANAGEMENT APPLICATIONS
Waino Suojanen, *Editor*

MANAGEMENT:
Ends and Means

R. W. Morell

University of South Florida

 CHANDLER PUBLISHING COMPANY

124 Spear Street

San Francisco, California 94105

 Science Research Associates, Inc., 259 East Erie Street, Chicago, Illinois 60611
A Subsidiary of IBM   Distributors

Contents

Figures

Preface

Much of the literature in the field of management has concentrated on the functional approach to management. A discussion of this approach usually begins with planning, includes the processes of organizing and giving directions or orders, and ends with the exercise of the controlling function. These functions represent the essence of management to the functionalists.

I have no quarrel with this traditional approach; on the contrary, it has focused attention upon many of the important fundamentals of management. On the other hand, the field of management is in a state of evolution which the functionalists cannot ignore. During World War II, with the advent of operations research, and since World War II management has been influenced by important advances in such disciplines as philosophy, psychology, sociology, logic, scientific method, and mathematics, all of which are directly related to management. Yet the contributions of these disciplines require some integration if they are to be useful to the manager. The integrative function necessary to make these contributions useful and to make the manager's knowledge useful in his daily administrative duties is the activity of decision-making: the cardinal and universal function of the manager.

The orientation of this book, then, is simply that the essence of management is a decision made by the manager through reasoning and in the light of what he knows. Good management is seen as good decision-making in real-world situations. Making a sound decision is a complex and difficult art; the intellectual processes involved require care, order, and step-by-step reasoning. If an individual cannot make sound decisions he cannot be a good manager regardless of the extent of his knowledge of the traditional functions of management or of the various disciplines related to management. Decision-making thus acts as the synthesizing force which makes a manager's knowledge useful as he applies that knowledge to his organization's problems.

This book emphasizes choice and the interdisciplinary areas upon which sound management must be based. The traditional functions of management are included but viewed as areas in which decisions are made. For in his day-to-day administrative activities, the manager does not say to himself that he is planning, that he is ready to commence organizing or directing, or that he is going to stop organizing and begin controlling: he simply makes decisions. He may make planning decisions, organizing decisions, directing decisions, and controlling decisions, yet he may not think of these decisions in terms of these functional areas, and whether or not he does will not alter the fact that what he does as a manager is make choices.

I hope that this volume will be useful to the student, to the teacher, and to the practitioner, and that the reader will be prompted to further study, discussion, and thought to secure a more comprehensive knowledge of the dynamic field of management. With this end in mind, discussion questions and selected references have been provided at the end of each chapter. In universities this book can be used as a basic text in courses in principles of management, organization theory, and management or administrative theory. It may also be used as a supplementary text in business policy, personnel management, or behavioral-science courses. Finally, organizations may find the book useful in their management-development programs.

R. W. MORELL

Tampa, Florida

MANAGEMENT:

Ends and Means

Chapter I

What Management Is

At twenty years of age, the will reigns; at thirty, the wit;
and at forty, the judgment.—BENJAMIN FRANKLIN

....

In order to give meaning to the phrase *"Management: Ends and
Means"* it is necessary to consider what is meant by the term
"management." The term "management" stems from the word
"manage" which, in turn, is derived from the French word
ménage, meaning "housekeeping." Thus, "management" in this
literal sense becomes the act of conducting the affairs of a household. Although we often speak of the management of a household, which is still the basic social and economic unit in society,
we use the term management in a much broader sense today.
Generally we use it in reference to a business, a hospital, an
educational institution, or some other kind of organization with
well defined goals to be achieved. In this sense, management deals
with the use of means or resources (personnel and property) by
an organization in an attempt to effectively achieve goals (something known and desired).

Various meanings have also been assigned to the term "management" by experts in management and in related fields. For example, the functionalists view management as consisting of three
or more activities or functions which usually include planning,
organizing, and controlling but may also include directing,
staffing and/or commanding, and, less often, coordinating. Behavioral scientists may view management as simply the process
of influencing human behavior or effecting organizational change.
The management systems expert may view it as a form of control of the organization in which the functions of management
and control become synonymous. The economist may view management as entrepreneurial, with resource allocation among com-

1

peting ends as the *raison d'être*. Indeed, some economists now present the factors of production as land, labor, capital, and management. The operations researcher has viewed management as a scientific application (quantitative-symbolic) to the selection of alternatives.

To the philosopher interested in discovering the steps an individual should take to achieve the goal of the good life, the classical conception of rationality was defined in terms of the ability to select means to achieve goals. This interpretation of the management of events in terms of the purpose to be fulfilled was what the Greek philosopher, Aristotle, in the fourth century B.C. called "final causes." These final causes are what we may now call "final goals," although the first to be known and desired were the last to be attained. All other goals are then appropriately called intermediate or proximate. Each of these last goals as they are achieved become means to a further goal until the final goal is reached. In addition to appreciating and accepting the philosopher's emphasis on ends and means, I also believe that the events of the last three decades in the development of management thought have further emphasized the significance of the activity of decision-making—that is, deciding among ends and among means. Since all managers must perform the function of decision-making, management is not adequately defined if decision-making is not included as an essential element.

For our purpose, then, management may be defined as follows: **Management is that activity in an organization which consists in deciding upon the ends (goals) of an organization and in deciding upon the means by which the goals are to be effectively reached.** This definition should be sufficiently broad to satisfy most critics, whether they be behavioral scientists, systems experts, operations researchers, economists, management theorists or practitioners, or even bureaucrats and functionalists. For what more comprehensive approach can one take than that of a philosopher in the investigation of the essence of management and its causality?

With the classical conception of rationality defined as the ability to select means to achieve goals, and with management defined as deciding upon the goals of an organization and the means by which the goals are to be reached, this book must be concerned with general questions such as: What does a manager do? Why is management an entity of its own? What is the nature of management? What is its area of activity and concern? What are the proper ends of organizations? What are the proper means of organizations? What is the nature of the environment within which management attempts to achieve goals? What are the significant values in management? What are the norms, standards, and criteria by which sound judgments of managers are to be determined?

A diffusive philosophical approach attempts to relate the meaning of management to the meaning of life by relating the goals and functions of organizations to the goals and functions of life. What managers do is dictated by the purpose of management, which in turn is dictated by what needs to be done in an organization. What needs to be done in an organization (functions or activities) is dictated by its ends or goals; the goals or ends of an organization are dictated by the needs of life; and the needs of life are dictated by the ends or goals of life. Thus, management as ends and means is concerned with what management ought to do as well as what it is actually doing. Accordingly, we must be concerned with the ultimate validation or justification of those activities that constitute management.

Chapter 2. The Ends and Means of Organizations

The Ends of Organizations
The Concept of Ends
Types of Goals
Ultimate Goals
The Financial Goal
The Employment Goal
The Return-to-Labor Goal
The Production Goal
Functional Goals
Purchasing Goals
Producing Goals
Marketing Goals
Financing Goals
Accounting Goals
Research and Development Goals
Facilitating Goals
Managing Goals
Immediate Goals
Job Goals
Task Goals
Motion Goals
Multiple Goals and Suboptimization

The Means of Organizations
The Concept of Means
Types of Means
External Means
Internal Means

Definition of an Organization

Discussion Questions

References

Chapter 2*

The Ends and Means of Organizations

> To manage men one ought to have a sharp mind
> in a velvet sheath.—GEORGE ELIOT

....

THE ENDS OF ORGANIZATIONS

The Concept of Ends

The term "end" has many synonyms. Here we shall use the terms *goal* and *objective* as synonymous with the term *end*. Although philosophers use the word "end" the most, people in management use the words "goal" and "objective" more frequently. Even though I shall use the word "goal" the most because of personal choice, the three terms shall be considered interchangeable and all three shall mean **something that is known and that is desired.** A goal thus requires an awareness of its existence as well as the desire to achieve it before it is sought by either an individual or an organization. But it is not sufficient merely to define "goal" to adequately understand its meaning and importance. An inquiry into the types of goals of individuals and organizations should deepen our insight into this significant concept.

Types of Goals

From a philosophical point of view, goals of both individuals and organizations seem naturally to be classifiable as follows: (1) ultimate, final, or enterprise; (2) intermediate or functional; and (3) proximate or immediate. Each of these classes may be further subdivided, and these categories and their subcategories require analysis.

---

* In Chapters 2 and 3, I recognize and appreciate the influence of the writing of Walter F. Gast, *Principles of Business Management* (St. Louis: St. Louis University, 1953), especially Chapters 1 and 2.

Ultimate Goals

Although ultimate or final goals are the last to be achieved, they are the ones which really initiate decisions and actions on the part of both individuals and organizations. Most people and all organizations have ultimate or more remote goals. The ultimate goals of individuals have been the subject of much discussion for many centuries. Many of us would say that happiness is the goal of the individual even though happiness cannot be measured. Of course, happiness need not be measurable to qualify as a goal. All that is necessary is that we aspire to some higher level of equilibrium or ideal situation. For example, one might strive for some level of perfection in himself even though he realizes that it can never actually be attained. Nevertheless, the attempt is justified on the grounds that some higher level of perfection will most certainly be achieved if an attempt is made.

Since organizations differ, as do individuals, it is natural to expect to find a considerable variety of ultimate goals contemplated or in existence. Moreover, the discussion of ultimate goals of the variety of organizations might become interminable if we attempted to examine the infinite possible number of different goals. Accordingly, we will not attempt to empirically examine the ultimate goals that organizations in practice attempt to achieve, but like the philosopher we shall be more concerned with what the goals of organizations ought to be to further the common good of society. One thing is certain: No organization will survive if it is dedicated only to self-preservation.[1] In the following discussion, we shall discover with pleasure that many organizations that we have personally observed are actually pursuing goals that they should be pursuing.

THE FINANCIAL GOAL

Of all the goals of organizations, especially business organizations, the most well known and most cited is *profit* or making money. To many people the term *business organization* immediately stirs up the image of profit and the profit seeker—a

---

[1] John A. Larson, ed., *The Responsible Businessman*, Readings from Fortune (New York: Holt, 1966), p. 254 of Louis Finkelstein's "The Businessman's Moral Failure."

seemingly nasty concept in some minds. That the public's concept of profit is somewhat inaccurate is made clear when we realize that the public's guess is that profits on sales are four times what they actually are.[2] Moreover, many people consider a large absolute dollar profit figure in the millions as "too much" profit, whereas the same figure expressed as a percentage of sales would be considered "reasonable," to say nothing of profit as a percentage of invested capital—the rate of return on investment. Such vague notions of profit demand that the subject be examined at length.

To begin with, the term "profit" does not mean the same to professionals who actually deal with profits. For example, the accountant has one concept and the economist has another. The costs and revenues reported by orthodox accounting are suited to the legal and financial purposes for which they were designed. Yet net profits as reported on the operating (profit and loss) statement does not measure economic profit. To the economist, the rewards to the factors of production are the following: (1) rent for land; (2) wage for labor; (3) interest for capital; and (4) profit for the entrepreneur. In the profit reward, the economist has in mind only that amount of profit necessary to compensate the risk taker for his service in foregoing consumption and in assuming risk. This may be called a "reasonable" return on the invested capital, or a "fair" or "just" return on the investment. The economist considers such reasonable profits a cost of doing business. Any profits in excess of this reasonable amount of return could thus be called "excess profits" or "pure profits." An organization must earn some minimum normal rate or return to keep its capital invested in a particular industry. The formation of capital takes place rapidly after the factors of production have received their rewards. A rate of return above or below the normal rate will indeed have significant short, intermediate, or long-run effects on resource allocation among industries in the economy. For instance, consumer purchases of television sets following World War II can be thought of as economic "ballots," with the resulting substantial profits thought of as election returns. The formation of capital in the television in-

[2] Claude Robinson, *Understanding Profits* (Princeton: Van Nostrand, 1961), pp. 30ff.

dustry via the excess profits route (retained earnings), and the flow of outside capital into that lucrative industry from other sources in the economy, are clear examples of the effect of profits on resource allocation. Conversely, if there had been losses instead of profits after World War II, there would have been no capital formation from profits (retained earnings) and no flow of outside capital into the television industry. As a result, economic resources would have flown away from the television industry and allocated to other more lucrative industries within the economy.

In the net profit figure reported by accountants, there is usually no inclusion of reasonable or normal profits as a *cost* in the calculation of net profit. Consequently, the accountant's net profit includes both normal profits and pure profits, if any. Since there is no formula by which the amount of pure profit can be calculated, nor an accounting technique by which normal profits can be separated from pure profits, we can conclude that the net income figure on the profit and loss statement does not measure economic income. It should be made clear immediately, however, that this is not to imply that profits as determined by conventional accounting methods should measure economic income, but rather to exemplify the divergence in the approaches of two professionals.

The above discussion of pure profit brings to mind another important question—that of the *justice*[3] of pure profits. Since pure profits represent rewards of an extraordinary nature over and above the normal profit that is necessary to keep capital invested in an organization, the demand that justice render each what is his due implies some limit to the amount of return that can be conferred upon investors. Excessive payments to investors or profit plowback of retained earnings by organizations for growth purposes could result in injustices, such as an inequitable distribution of the fruits of production to the factors of production. The idea of "limit," however, brings up the question of "how much"? Since pure profit cannot be calculated, how can

[3] Justice refers to the disposition or willingness of men to do what is right, just, or equitable, or what is due to others. A more extended treatment of justice is presented in Chapter 4.

anyone determine how much pure profit, if any, there is in a given fiscal period of an organization? The answer is quite simple. When quantitative or objective means are not available, men frequently use qualitative or subjective means. That is, since it is not possible to calculate pure profits, it is certainly possible to form a *judgment* about the "limits." Men are adept at making judgments about all kinds of things, frequently in areas where they are not actually qualified to do so. Therefore, since judgment-making is such a universal activity, I see no reason why judgments cannot be made with respect to the question of "how much pure profit is too much pure profit." Of course, such a judgment must consider the fact that the rate of return on invested capital must be conditioned by the risk which investors assume. As the risk of any investment increases, the normal rate of return to compensate for such risk should likewise increase, and conversely.

With respect to the concept of profit, I wish to take the position that the significant concept is not the absolute dollar figure of net profit, but rather the ratio of the net profit to the equity capital invested in the organization. This ratio is called the rate of return on capital, the rate of return on investment, or the profit yield on capital or investment. Thus, if an organization earned $18 million net profit after taxes with an invested capital of $300 million, the rate of return would be $18 million divided by $300 million, or a rate of 6 per cent. An organization must earn some minimum rate to keep its capital invested in a particular industry.

A corollary question of some importance revolves around nonprofit organizations such as hospitals and educational institutions. The basic objective for the existence of such organizations is not the realization of profits but the provision of services that are useful and socially desirable. Such nonprofit organizations rely to a certain extent on endowments, gifts, fund raising, and certain assessments which are needed to keep the organization going. Nevertheless, I cannot agree that such present-day organizations are not interested in profits or income at all. A good example is the hospital industry. There the belief exists that endowments and gifts are expected to be less plentiful in the future,[4] especially in a society in which it is becoming more difficult to amass large fortunes. Under such conditions hospitals must give more attention to improved hospital management, hospital finance, and hospital accounting. Since World War II the accountant has become significantly more important to hospitals, and recognition of the need for putting hospitals on a more businesslike basis under the direction of a qualified administrator has led to the organization of curricula in hospital administration in a number of universities. The fact that many hospitals are organized as nonprofit corporations does not preclude a hospital from earning income; rather, the hospital must not distribute its income as stated, for example, in the statute of the State of Illinois as follows:

" 'Not for Profit Corporation' means a corporation no part of the income of which is distributable to its members, directors or officers; provided, however, that the payment of reasonable compensation for services rendered and the making of distributions upon dissolution or final liquidation as permitted by this Act, shall not be deemed a distribution of income."[5]

Moreover, the terms "gross income from patients," "net income from patients," and "other revenue" appear on a hospital's statement of income and expense. The last item of the operating statement is, however, never called "net income" or "net loss" but usually "excess of income over expense" or "excess of expense over income." I do not believe that calling the hospital's net income "excess of income over expense" changes the nature of the item—it is still net income regardless of the phrase used. Such "excess of income over expense" can be retained in hospitals for expansion purposes just as it can in a business organization. I am not at all opposed to hospitals or any other nonprofit organizations earning income. But since many people who do not fully understand the situation level charges at the "profit-mongering" business organizations, it is necessary to point out that many nonprofit corporations earn income, and rightly so. The only

4 T. Leroy Martin, *Hospital Accounting*, 4th ed. (Chicago: Physician's Record Co., 1964), p. 1.
5 Illinois General Not-for-Profit Corporation Act, approved July 17, 1948, Section 1, paragraph 2.

difference is that corporations organized for profit may distribute their income as dividends, whereas nonprofit corporations may not.

THE EMPLOYMENT GOAL

The foregoing financial goal of profit and rate of return is known to most people as a goal of organizations; no one argues that organizations are not interested in profits. Debate could arise, however, over whether or not an organization has any obligation to concern itself with a public matter such as employment, especially among minority groups. Emphasis on the primacy of the profit motive began with Adam Smith's insight into competition in a profit-and-loss economy. Classical economic theory—from Smith through John Stuart Mill to Alfred Marshall —never really appreciated the difference between a factory system composed of large corporations and an atomistic economy which rested solely on market mechanisms. Even now some economists such as F. A. Hayek still feel that managers must be concerned with the single task of using the available capital to maximize profits.[6] On the other hand, advocates of corporate social responsibility feel that an organization is as much a social and political entity as it is an economic entity. The Harvard economist, John Kenneth Galbraith, points out that the traditional assumptions of orthodox economic theory no longer fit the facts: (1) the giant corporate complexes in the United States today have blurred the old demarcation between private and public; (2) the success or failure of these corporate complexes is no longer determined in a competitive consumer-controlled market—the corporations determine what is to be produced at what prices; (3) the primary corporate incentive is no longer the maximization of profits, but growth; (4) the economic system is not self-balancing.[7] In December 1964, Keith Davis, in his presidential address to the Academy of Management meeting in Chicago, insisted that management's responsibilities extend be-

[6] F. A. Hayek, "The Corporation in a Democratic Society," *Management and Corporations, 1985,* Melvin Anshen and George L. Bach, ed. (New York: McGraw-Hill, 1960) , pp. 99-100.

[7] John K. Galbraith, *The New Industrial State* (Boston: Houghton Mifflin, 1967) , Chapters 1, 5, 28, 30, 35.

yond the organization's interest in profit to include community values and general welfare.[8]

The changing role of organizations in the socioeconomic sense, the affluency that has followed World War II, the separation of ownership and control (by professional managers) within the modern organizations, and recent civil-rights legislation should tip the scales in favor of some "enlightened self-interest" on the part of the leaders of industry. This enlightenment should motivate them to reexamine their views on the social responsibilities of their organizations.

Who, then, is responsible for providing employment opportunities? In my opinion the responsibility for providing and maintaining employment belongs to the leaders of profit and nonprofit organizations. To say that employment is not a concern of organizations is tantamount to saying that we should have more government intervention or social control. In this connection, managers of organizations are very much involved whether they are ready for it or not, for one demand of the civil-rights movement is for "equal employment opportunities" in the midst of affluency.[9] On July 2, 1964 Congress passed the Civil Rights Act of 1964. Title VII of the Act, "Equal Employment Opportunity," prohibits discrimination in hiring, upgrading, and all other conditions of employment. It became effective on July 2, 1965. Title VII established the Equal Employment Opportunity Commission composed of five members appointed by the President and approved by the Senate. The Commission's responsibility is to assure that all Americans will be considered for hiring and promotion on the basis of their ability and qualifications, without regard to race, color, religion, sex, or national origin. It is fortunate that a growing number of administrators, executives, and managers have a deep conviction that employment must be an ultimate goal of organizations, coordinate with the financial goal, and these same sensitive leaders have shown a profound concern over

[8] Keith Davis, "The Public Role of Management," Edwin Flippo, ed., *Evolving Concepts in Management: Proceedings of the 24th Annual Meeting* (University Park: Academy of Management, 1965), p. 6.

[9] Larson, ed., *The Responsible Businessman*. See especially Part 3, "Business and the Negro," and Part 4, "Poverty as a Business Problem" for extended discussions of the employment and poverty problems.

the social consequences of failure to regard employment as such a goal. "Jobs are the live ammunition in the war on poverty," says Secretary of Labor Willard Wirtz. And, he adds, it's up to business and industry to pass the ammunition.[10]

THE RETURN-TO-LABOR GOAL

Whether or not employment is acceptable to the reader as an ultimate goal of organizations, there will probably be much less opposition to the concept of a living wage for labor or to the provision of opportunities by organizations for personal satisfactions by employees on the job. Let us now turn to the concept of a living wage.

There should be no need to justify a living wage to labor for its services to the organization. Yet there are skeptical theorists and practitioners who would actually pay labor as little as possible, even though the recipient and his family could not live on his wages.

First, the wage earner (any person whose time and efforts are directly involved in the operation of an organization) has a natural right to a living wage because he has a right to live. The right to live is one of the most basic rights of mankind protected by the state. But in a money economy, the laborer's right to live is dependent upon his receiving a living wage. Since the right to a living wage is a fundamental human right, the next question is: What is a living wage? **A living wage is a wage paid to the worker that is sufficient to support him and his family.** Among the things due a worker are: housing, food, clothing, some property, some education, some minimum level of health and other ordinary family needs, some cultural and/or recreational pursuits, and certain social appurtenances dependent upon his status in society. Moreover, the wage should be sufficient so that the mother[11] or the children should not have to work. Finally, a man should receive enough from his wages during his produc-

---

[10] Editors of McGraw-Hill, "Business and the Urban Crisis," *Electrical Construction and Maintenance,* Vol. 67, No. 2, February, 1968, C5.

[11] I am aware that there are many working wives in the United States. This situation is fine. However, if there are children they usually suffer if they are deprived of their mother's care during their formative years, except in special cases where the mother may be in poor physical or mental health.

tive years so that he need not fear economic insecurity in his old age. It does not seem unreasonable to me that industry should bear some of the cost of supporting the retired worker when during his most productive years industry willingly took the fruits of his work which, when combined with the other factors of production, permitted some distribution to all of the factors. In this connection, the Social Security Act of 1935 and the Older Americans Act of 1965 should help to supplement industry's contribution to the economic problem of aging.

On the other hand, the demand of the living wage is not unequivocal or without conditions. Supplying a sufficient wage to provide the worker with his basic needs according to his station in life depends, of course, upon the value of his productive services to the organization. Within the limits of productivity, an employee deserves a wage which approximates the value of his services as closely as possible. Thus, the worker has the responsibility to be as productive as possible, while at the same time the organization has the obligation to provide the means to enable him to attain a desirable level of productiveness. Yet if an organization finds it impossible to pay a living wage because of some maladjustment within the economy, within the industry, or within the firm, the employers and employees should cooperatively attempt to alleviate the situation aided by government measures.[12] Finally, unusual circumstances may require payment of very high wages to certain professionals in an organization who render a service that is scarce and that contributes much to the output and/or reputation of the organization.

But man does not live by bread alone. This statement indirectly points out that man is a social animal and that his economic activity in an organization is a social endeavor. Consequently, he does not have only monetary or material needs. Our next

---

[12] In the fall of 1966, Congress passed Public Law No. 89-601, the "Fair Labor Standards Amendments of 1966." The law went into effect on February 1, 1967 and establishes minimum wage provisions and overtime provisions on consecutive first days of February. Although this Federal Wage & Hour Law provides for certain exempt employees, nevertheless the creation of a minimum wage by law seems to be moving in the direction of a living wage. Moreover, almost 300 Federal mediators are now employed to act as persuaders in labor negotiations on wages, hours, and other management-labor matters.

subject is the important matter of the provision of opportunities by organizations for their employees' personal satisfactions.

To say that man is a very complex organism is one thing, but to begin to spell out some of these complexities as they affect the work situation, which we shall briefly attempt here, is quite another. To begin with, while there are many similarities among people, no two individuals are exactly alike. An individual's job expectations are influenced by many things—heredity, environment, education, experience, sex, age, physical condition, psychological characteristics, and sociological factors such as culture, social class, and customs. Since an individual spends most of his waking hours at his job, he naturally expects to express his personality while at work. If a job situation does not permit this expression, work becomes a repressive and frustrating experience rather than a stimulating one. In extreme cases, an individual may become maladjusted.

What does an individual look for from a job, other than monetary reward? Psychologists provide some answers to this question, though we must realize that they also differ in identifying human needs and desires. A. H. Maslow[13] has developed a widely accepted hierarchy of human needs as follows:

1. Physiological needs
2. Safety needs
3. Love (social needs)
4. Esteem (ego needs)
5. Self-actualization (self-fulfillment needs)

Another widely accepted list of human needs is presented by Douglas McGregor in three categories: (1) physical—the need for food, shelter, rest; (2) social—the need for companionship, acceptance; and (3) ego—the need for a sense of achievement, self-respect.[14] Since the Maslow need hierarchy encompasses the

[13] A. H. Maslow, "A Theory of Human Motivation," *Psychological Review*, Vol. 50, July 1943, pp. 370-396.
[14] Douglas McGregor, "The Supervisor's Job." Address before the Management Forum, E. I. Dupont de Nemours & Co., Inc., Wilmington, Delaware, April 16, 1948. See also Douglas McGregor's *The Human Side of Enterprise* (New York: McGraw-Hill, 1960), pp. 36-39, for a summary of Maslow's need hierarchy. For a critique of management's approach and the presentation of ideas for improvement (Theory X and Theory Y), see Chapters 3, 4.

McGregor list, let us examine the Maslow hierarchy in some detail.

This discussion began with the statement that "man does not live by bread alone." While this statement is true, man does live for bread alone when there is no bread. In other words, as Maslow envisions it, "higher needs"—those numbered 2, 3, 4, and 5 above—become activated only if the "lower" ones—the basic physiological needs—become satisfied. Thus, an individual's social needs and ego needs are inoperative when his stomach is empty. A generalization is now possible: A satisfied need does not motivate behavior; conversely, an unsatisfied need does motivate behavior.

Once man's physiological needs are reasonably satisfied, he becomes aware of certain other unsatisfied needs. In Maslow's construct, safety needs are the next group of needs requiring satisfaction. Safety needs are the needs for protection gainst threat and deprivation. Arbitrary management actions, unwise policy statements, inept policy administration, favoritism, inequitable decisions, discrimination, and the like stimulate the safety needs in the dependent employment relationship.

With the physiological and safety needs satisfied, one's social needs (love) become important according to Maslow's structure. The desire for friendship and affection and the need for association with others constitute one's social needs. When, in his view, an individual's social and safety needs are thwarted, his organizational behavior may become antagonistic and uncooperative as a consequence of the deprivation.

Next in order above the social needs are the ego needs, which may be broadly classified as self-esteem and reputation. The former relate to the needs for self-confidence, achievement, and knowledge; the latter relate to the needs for status, recognition, and appreciation. Unlike the lower needs, the ego needs are rarely satisfied, especially at lower organizational levels. At higher organizational levels, as one moves away from the production-centered situation, ego needs should have increased opportunities for gratification. But even here the level of satiation is something less than inspiring.

Finally, at the crest, are the self-fulfillment needs—the needs for self-development and the realization of one's own potentialities. We can see that modern life, especially with man's pre-occupation with making a living, provides only limited opportunity for the expression of ego needs. Nevertheless, the needs exist and management should try to meet the challenge of helping people express them.

The above classification of people's needs and desires helps to explain some of management's mistakes in the treatment of employees. People in the management field such as Mary Parker Follett, Elton Mayo, and Chris Argyris join with John Coleman Bennett and Reinhold Niebuhr in the Protestant tradition; Pope Leo XIII and Pope Pius XI in the Catholic tradition; and Rabbi Abraham Heschel, David Ponitz, and Rabbi Lewis Finkelstein in the Judaic tradition to urge managers to consider the dignity of the individual who has basic needs and who should not be treated as an automaton in a machine culture.[15] Such laws as the Wagner and Taft-Hartley Acts, the Social Security Acts, the Fair Labor Standards Act, and the Civil Rights Act, which dictate certain minimum standards of treatment, show that society has not generally approved of management's treatment of its employees. Personal satisfaction on the job cannot thus be completely provided by a pay check. The problem of providing opportunities for personal satisfactions on the job can be solved only by the willingness of managers to see the inescapable logic of accepting responsibility for providing satisfying job situations, not only because it will obviously mean lower costs and greater efficiency and output, but also because it is something which the employees need and is due them as part of the "return to labor."

THE PRODUCTION GOAL

We have now examined at length the following goals of an organization: (1) the financial goal; (2) the employment goal; and (3) the return-to-labor goal. If the organization is to accept these three goals, it must then dedicate itself to the economical use of its labor and its capital in order to produce a want-satisfying good and/or service. This is the fourth and final ultimate goal of any organization—the production goal.

---

[15] Clarence C. Walton, *Corporate Social Responsibilities* (Belmont: Wadsworth, 1967), p. 130.

The managers of any legitimate organization will readily agree that organizations must produce, but many will more likely think of production as a means to some end such as profit and not as an end in itself. The notion of production as one of the ultimate or final ends of organizations may strike them as largely academic and impractical. This is more true of managers of profit organizations than it is of managers of nonprofit organizations. For instance, it is quite common for a hospital administrator or an educational administrator to list the services produced by their hospitals and their educational institutions as ultimate goals. Thus, the hospital administrator thinks and speaks of "care of the patient" as an ultimate goal while the educational administrator thinks and speaks of "service to the student" as an ultimate goal.

In a capitalistic economic system dedicated to the proposition that the wants and desires of its citizens should be satisfied primarily by private means rather than by social means, individuals may lose confidence if private enterprise does not provide for the satisfaction of the wants of society. It simply becomes a matter of justice for organizations to accept production of a want-satisfying commodity and/or service as a goal for the common good of society.[16] Anything less could lead, in the extreme, to the destruction of economic life as we now know it in the United States. Moreover, the efficient and economical use of labor and capital by organizations implies usage with a deliberate attempt to secure as much product and/or service as possible. For what is an organization if it is not an instrument for the production of a want-satisfying commodity and/or service? An organization exists primarily to produce goods or services as efficiently as possible. Finally, in pursuing the objective of production by economical means, organizations must also seek to achieve the other ultimate goals of employment, the return to labor, and the financial goal.

[16] The farm problem is a classic example of abuse in the economic system because of the nonacceptance of the production of a want-satisfying commodity as a goal. Government price supports for certain agricultural products led to excessive overproduction of commodities not of the want-satisfying type. As a result, it cost the taxpayers around one million dollars per day just to store these commodities under government control.

Functional Goals

The foregoing analysis of ultimate goals should have established their importance since ultimate goals are the reasons for the existence of organizations. If organizations could not achieve ultimate goals better than individuals operating alone could, there would be little reason for their existence. The millions of successful organizations in the United States prove that many organizations must be adequately achieving their ultimate goals. In attempting to achieve these ultimate goals, organizations usually set somewhat lesser goals—intermediate or functional— to be achieved. **Functional goals are thus decisions from among alternative ends made in the belief that they will serve as the means of achieving some of the ultimate goals.** In the classification of goals, it should be kept in mind that there is no universal classification system with which everyone or every organization would agree.[17] Some people would call certain of the above named ultimate goals intermediate and some would call some of the following functional goals ultimate. This is because the choices of goals are significantly influenced by the varying backgrounds and accumulated experiences of the decision-maker. Since each person has a different conceptual structure or framework of ideas, decisions about goals are subjective decisions; that is, such decisions are measured by one's personal standards rather than by objective standards. Nevertheless, some position must be taken here in order to analyze the concept of clear-cut goals. Accordingly, I realize that the approach taken in this chapter is not the only approach, but it is the one I believe in.

PURCHASING GOALS

The operating functions or activities of an organization include purchasing, producing, marketing, financing, accounting, research and development, and facilitating. Each one of these functions has its own goals, hence the term "functional goals." For example, the purchasing function should have the following stated goals: (1) the maintenance of the continuity of operations;

[17] See Manley Howe Jones, *Executive Decision-Making* (Homewood: Irwin, 1957) , Chapter I, for another classification of goals.

(2) the maintenance of adequate standards of quality; (3) the avoidance of duplication, waste, and obsolescence; (4) the maintenance of the organization's competitive position; and (5) the development of internal relationships that lead to understanding and harmony among the organizational units of an enterprise.[18] In connection with the maintenance of the continuity of operations, the function of purchasing must be so conducted as to minimize disruptions in production resulting from the lack of materials, equipment, or supplies, and with a minimum investment in inventories. With respect to the maintenance of adequate standards of quality, the objective is to procure goods that are best suited at the lowest cost rather than those goods of the highest quality. The avoidance of duplication, waste, and obsolescence requires that each purchase be considered in terms of long-range and short-range plans which give rise to the purchase. The maintenance of the organization's competitive position requires that the purchasing agent make sure that quality standards do not exceed those of competitors'. Finally, since the purchasing agent buys everything from pencils to factories for all the divisions and departments in the organization, he must exercise leadership to develop understanding and harmony among the units within the organization.

PRODUCING GOALS

Another operating function of an organization is producing, which involves the creation of *form* utility. Utility means the capacity to satisfy wants. Producing actually refers, then, to that operating function of an organization which creates goods and services. The goals of the producing function may be stated thus: (1) to create the prescribed product (s) and/or service (s) ; (2) to create the right quantity of the prescribed product (s) and/or service (s) at the right time; (3) to use all capital assets with maximum economy (maximum effectiveness, minimum idleness, and minimum perishability) ; (4) to use all materials, parts, and supplies with maximum economy and a minimum of waste; (5) to use labor with maximum justice and maximum economy; and (6) to strive for a minimum of labor, material,

18 J. H. Westing, I. V. Fine, and Members of the Milwaukee Association of Purchasing Agents, *Industrial Purchasing* (New York: Wiley, 1955), pp. 6-7.

and overhead costs consistent with established standards of quality of product (s) and/or service (s). These goals need little comment since they are almost self-explanatory. In reference to number (6), however, the three elements of cost commonly known as material, labor, and overhead include all items of fixed, semivariable, and variable expense involved with the producing function. Finally, the term "overhead" has many synonyms. It has been called burden, indirect expense, fixed expense, factory expense, and manufacturing expense. The last two terms apply only to industrial or manufacturing organizations. The other four terms of overhead, burden, fixed expense, and indirect expense are relevant to all organizations.

MARKETING GOALS

The function of marketing may be defined as "the economic process by means of which goods and services are exchanged and their values determined in terms of money prices."[19] As such, marketing embraces all business activities involved in the movement of goods and services from production to consumption. To realize the importance of marketing in the economy, it is only necessary to state the goals of the marketing function: (1) to dispose of all the products and services of the economy at reasonable prices, with the least difficulty, and with a minimum of waste and cost; (2) to predetermine through market research and analysis what goods and services should be created; (3) to influence in some way the demand for goods and services; and (4) to provide a marketing system sufficiently flexible so that it may be readily adapted to the changing wants of consumers and the fluctuating varieties of goods and services.[20] The distribution of goods and services through the marketing function to consumers gives rise to what is known as *place, time,* and *ownership* utilities. Whereas the producing function gives rise to *form* utility, as stated above, the marketing function adds place, time, and ownership utilities to goods and services, thereby making goods much more valuable to the consumer because he

[19] Edward A. Duddy and David A. Revzan, *Marketing* (New York: McGraw-Hill, 1947), p. 4.

[20] Harold H. Maynard and Theodore N. Beckman, *Principles of Marketing*, 4th ed. (New York: Ronald, 1946), p. 21.

can go to an organization such as a retail store (place) on April 3 (time) and actually buy (ownership) a suit. Also, a patient can go to a hospital (place) on May 5 (time) and buy (ownership) medical care. The second objective attempts to minimize or eliminate the waste of producing and marketing goods and services that are not want satisfying, while the third goal of the marketing function attempts to increase the total demand in the economy by sales promotion, especially advertising. Finally, since the consumer of goods and services is king, the marketing system must be ready to respond to his changing needs and desires—the fourth goal of the marketing function.

FINANCING GOALS

A fourth operating function of an organization is financing. Financing consists of obtaining and effectively utilizing the funds or assets necessary for efficient operation of an organization. Fundamentally, the goals of the financing function are (1) to see that the cash is on hand to pay bills on time, and (2) to assist in the maximization of the long-run profits of the firm.[21] In attempting to achieve these two important goals, the financial executive faces a dilemma. In order to effectively assist in the creation of earnings for his organization, the financial officer ideally would prefer to have the firm's funds invested in inventory, capital equipment, accounts receivable, or any asset other than cash, especially since cash is the only asset that earns nothing. On the other hand, the need to meet bills and debts on time so that the organization's credit reputation will not be damaged requires maintaining a minimum level of liquidity. In obtaining the funds for the organization, the treasurer must be concerned about the cost of the funds to the organization, the conditions under which they can be obtained in the money and capital markets, and the period of time involved. The distinction between short-term financing, intermediate-term financing, and long-term financing now becomes significant. Finally, once the funds have been obtained, financial analysis and investment analysis must contribute to the effective use of the funds if the two objectives cited above are to be achieved satisfactorily.

[21] Robert W. Johnson, *Financial Management* (Boston: Allyn & Bacon, 1959), p. 11.

ACCOUNTING GOALS

The fifth operating function of an organization is the accounting function. The accounting function and the financing function are closely related but are quite different functions. Although both accounting and financing use similar terminology, accounting is clearly defined by the American Institute of Certified Public Accountants as ". . . the art of recording, classifying, and summarizing in a significant manner and in terms of money, transactions and events which are, in part at least, of a financial character, and interpreting the results thereof."[22] Thus, accounting is concerned with the recording, classifying, summarizing, and interpreting of transactions and their expression in monetary terms, while financing is concerned with the acquisition and utilization of funds. Basically, the primary goal of accounting is the objective provision of financial information for stockholders, management, banks and other creditors, and government agencies. More specifically, the goals of the accounting function may be stated as follows: (1) to determine net income; (2) to facilitate administrative control; and (3) to determine taxable income.[23] The problem of income determination implies the objective disclosure of revenue, costs, and expenses as well as the status of assets and equities and the preparation and interpretation of financial statements. The facilitation of administrative control envisions the role of accounting data as a useful quantitative tool of management. Here the goal is to provide management with data, as do the statistician, the economist, and the mathematician, which are useful in making managerial decisions. Finally, since the determination of taxable income is so important today in so many profit-oriented organizations, and because the measurement of taxable income depends largely upon accounting data for its accurate calculation, it seems reasonable to consider it an objective of the accounting function, realizing that only goals (1) and (2) would be relevant goals for nonprofit organizations.

[22] *Accounting Terminology Bulletin Number 1, Review & Resume* (New York: American Institute of Certified Public Accountants, Committee on Terminology, 1953) , p. 9.

[23] C. Aubrey Smith and J. G. Ashburne, *Financial and Administrative Accounting*, 2nd ed. (New York: McGraw-Hill, 1960) , pp. 10-11.

RESEARCH AND DEVELOPMENT GOALS

The sixth operating function of an organization is research and development. Prior to World War II, organizations tended to view systematic research and development with skepticism. As a matter of fact, research and development was looked upon as an extremely risky and very expensive function. But the period after World War II changed this view. Indeed, World War II and the affluent society following World War II, in which the demand for any product or service may vanish quickly because of substitution, began to change some of the traditional thinking about research and development. Management began to view research and development as an essential aspect of survival and growth in a dynamic economy. Research and development not only became a defensive measure, but organizations also began to realize that changes initiated within the organization were more manageable than changes initiated outside the organization.[24] Although some corporations often have vague purposes and amorphous goals, one thing is certain: Research and development is inconceivable unless it is goal-oriented. What are the goals of research and development? The goal of research is an intellectual one of discovery and understanding, whereas the goal of development is a practical (operational) one of devising new choices for human action.[25] The purpose of the latter is to put the new product, device, service, process, or technique into a form in which it can be sold and/or used.[26]

FACILITATING GOALS

The final operating function of an organization is the facilitating function. The facilitating function includes all activities which aid or support the operating functions of purchasing, producing, marketing, financing, accounting, research and development, and the managing functions. The facilitating function thus becomes something of a catch-all category. That is, those

[24] Waino Suojanen, *The Dynamics of Management* (New York: Holt, 1966), pp. 85-86, 118, 140-141.

[25] Cyril O'Donnell *et al.*, *The Strategy of Corporate Research, A Symposium* (San Francisco: Chandler, 1967) see p. 190ff. of "The Strategy of Corporate Research and Development" by R. E. Gibson.

[26] Suojanen, *The Dynamics of Management*, p. 30.

activities in an organization which do not fit into purchasing, producing, marketing, financing, accounting, research and development, or managing may be considered facilitating. Examples include maintenance, legal aid, policing, and clerical work. Facilitating functions have no special goals of their own but rather take on the goals of the operating or managing functions. For instance, the goals of the facilitating function of factory maintenance work would be the goals of producing, or the facilitating function of clerical work in the purchasing department would have the goals of the purchasing function. If the clerical activities were being performed to aid a manager engaged in planning, the goals of the facilitating function would be the goals of the planning function (to be discussed in the next section). The same may be said for any facilitating function serving any operating or any managing function.

MANAGING GOALS

The managing functions are entirely different from the operating functions of an organization. What the managers of an organization actually manage is the personnel and capital functioning in the operating functions of purchasing, producing, marketing, financing, accounting, research and development, and facilitating. The managing of purchasing must thus never be confused with purchasing, nor the managing of producing with producing, nor the managing of marketing with marketing, nor the managing of financing with financing, nor the managing of accounting with accounting, nor the managing of research and development with research and development, nor the managing of facilitating with facilitating. This differentiation is attested to by the fact that each of the operating functions has its own goals as described above, while each of the managing functions has its own goals. And the goals of the operating functions are different from the goals of the managing functions. The managing of the personnel and capital engaged in the operating functions is the reason management exists. Whereas the fundamental responsibility of management is to see that all the goals of an organization are achieved, the specific functions of managing each have their own goals. Thus, the goal of managerial decision-making is to make sound decisions. And if we use the traditional functions for a moment, the goal of planning is to make good plans; the goal of organizing is a stable, yet flexible, organization; the goal of directing is motivated direction; and the goal of controlling is control. The concept of management and the separation of the operating and managing functions will take on considerably more meaning as the reader pursues the matter in greater detail in Chapter 4, the Nature of Management.

Immediate Goals

The preceding examination of functional goals discussed the objectives peculiar to the particular operating or managing function. While the goals of any particular function are not necessarily shared by other functions, the goals of each operating and managing function are set up on the belief that they will contribute to the achievement of the common objectives of an organization—the ultimate goals. Since the ultimate goals and the functional goals have been treated at length, it is now necessary to examine the final category of goals of an organization—the immediate goals. For this purpose immediate goals may be subdivided as follows: (1) job goals; (2) task goals; (3) motion goals.

JOB GOALS

Since functions are broad classes of activities, in order to achieve the goals of particular functions it is necessary to divide these classes into subordinate work units. These units are called jobs. **A job is a specific amount of work to be performed by one person or one piece of capital.** For a job to contribute to the achievement of the functional and the ultimate goals of an organization, it must have a purpose. This purpose is the expression of the specific goals of the job, and these goals are not to be confused with the duties of a job. What a person actually does on a job are his duties, but the goals are the reasons why he engages in these duties. Let us take as an example the stenographer's job. While a stenographer may perform many duties such as taking dictation in shorthand, transcribing dictated material, filing, and the like, the goals of the stenographer's job in this case would be (1) the maintenance of a high level of accurately transcribed material and (2) the maintenance of an orderly condition of the files. Every duty the stenographer performs should directly or indirectly contribute to the achievement of one or both of these two goals. The same thing can be said for any job. Each job has its duties and its goals and the two should be kept clearly and distinctly in mind.

TASK GOALS

A job as a specific amount of work is composed of elements known as tasks. **A task is a part of a job.** The aforementioned stenographer's duties may thus be referred to as tasks. Each task in turn has its own objectives. The task of filing material alphabetically or according to index number is done to achieve the goal of "prompt deposit of written material." The achievement of this goal would, in turn, contribute to the achievement of goal (2) of the stenographer's job as mentioned above—the maintenance of an orderly condition of the files. But the orderly condition of the files is also affected by the withdrawal of materials from the files. If material is withdrawn and not refiled promptly or misfiled, an orderly condition of the files will not exist despite the fact that "prompt deposit of written material" was initially achieved with respect to the withdrawn material. All the other tasks of a stenographer similarly have their goals. The more aware the employees are of goals of a job and goals of tasks, the more meaningful the job and tasks will be for them.

MOTION GOALS

The final type of immediate goal is the motion goal. A job is made up of tasks, and similarly, a task is made up of motions. **A motion may be considered as any movement necessary to perform a task.** Like jobs and tasks, motions also have purpose. To continue the example of the stenographer, the task of filing requires a number of motions. For example, the stenographer must pull out the drawers of a file. The objective in pulling out the drawers of a file is "to gain access to the written material." Prompt deposit or withdrawal of material or the maintenance of an orderly condition of the files will not be possible unless the stenographer frequently pulls open the drawers of the file. Thus we see that each motion which makes up a task must have its own goal or purpose. The fact that some motions are apparently without purpose and have no relation to particular tasks has made *motion study* important as a means of eliminating unnecessary motions, and minimizing and ordering necessary ones.

Multiple Goals and Suboptimization

The foregoing discussion of goals was presented by proceeding from the most general goals to the most specific. By class, ultimate goals were followed by functional goals which were followed by immediate goals. This structure is a *hierarchy of goals* with ultimate goals at the top, immediate goals at the bottom, and functional goals in between. The conception of goals in a vertical sense is only part of the story. At each horizontal level we found a number of goals. At the ultimate goal level there is the financial goal, the employment goal, the return to labor goal, and the production goal. At the functional level there are several goals for each function, and at the immediate goal level there are the job goals, the task goals, and the motion goals (see Figure 2-1). It is quite obvious, therefore, that an organization is faced with *multiple goals,* which create problems.

Any organization that believes in its goals will usually attempt to optimize its situation by striving for a maximum achievement of its goals. When there are multiple goals, **the optimization of one goal can frequently result in a lower degree of attainment or achievement of one or more other goals. This state or condition is known as suboptimization.**[27] For example, in the area of ultimate goals, to obtain some level of achievement of the financial goal the organization may short change any one or all of the other ultimate goals. Or it may be desirable in an organization to develop departments along functional lines. Such departments are likely to possess a good deal of autonomy, which may lead to one department's attempting to achieve certain functional or departmental goals to the detriment of certain other departments and, in some cases, even to the entire organization. Moreover, the achievement of objectives takes

[27] David W. Miller and Martin K. Starr, *Executive Decisions and Operations Research* (Englewood Cliffs: Prentice-Hall, 1960), p. 40.

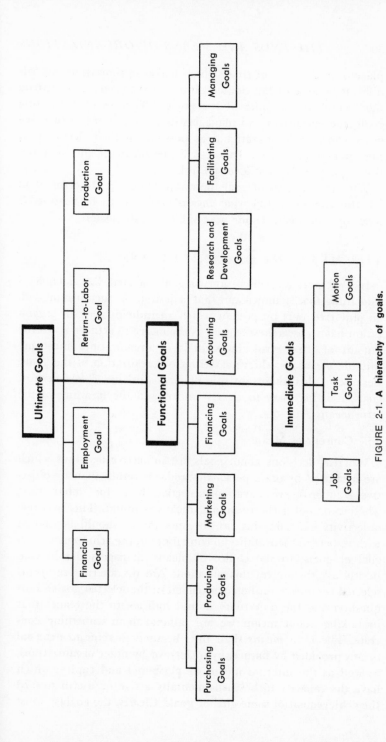

FIGURE 2-1. A hierarchy of goals.

place over a period of time, which makes optimization of goals difficult because of the limited ability of managers to anticipate the future. Yet in spite of the great difficulties of optimizing goals, the executives and managers of organizations must make every effort to be as rational as possible in their decisions in the attempt to reach a balanced achievement of the organization's goals at the best level possible.

With the analysis of goals now terminated, it is pertinent to ask this question: "By what means are goals to be achieved"? The topic of means is our next subject of discussion.

THE MEANS OF ORGANIZATIONS

In the preceding discussion of goals, a goal was defined as something that is known and that is desired. As such it is an end, an objective, or a purpose of which an individual or an organization has an awareness as well as the desire to achieve it. In the pursuit of these goals, individuals or organizations must use suitable means to achieve a satisfactory realization of the goals. Because of this important role of means in the achievement of goals, it is necessary to clearly understand the meaning of the term *means*.

The Concept of Means

Whereas decisions about goals are subjective decisions which are measured by one's personal standards rather than by objective standards, we have an objective basis for determining whether or not a choice among means is sound. This welcome objectivity exists in this case because means should be chosen with respect to their ability to contribute to the achievement of a goal or goals. In the choice of means, managers should constantly ask themselves this question: Are the alternative means selected conducive to the achievement of the selected goals? This question and the objectivity should indicate to the reader that in talking about means we are talking about something concrete. The term *means* shall thus be used to **refer to external means provided by nature, by society, or by other organizations, as well as the internal means of personnel and capital which have the capacity to be instrumentally active or useful toward the achievement of some goal or goals.** Clearly, the goal (s) must first be known before the specific means can be intelligently selected. It should now be quite clear why this chapter first covered goals before considering means. Although obvious to the reader, the precedence of goals over means is not as obvious to many people. Some people in organizations waste considerable effort because they do not seem to know precisely what their goals are. These people frequently appear as bundles of energy and activity that lack direction, which could be easily supplied by clear-cut goals. To more deeply appreciate the meaning and importance of means, let us now turn to the types of means.

Types of Means

The means of organizations may be classified as (1) external and (2) internal. The external means are those which lie outside the confines of the organization, and are those which are provided by nature, by society, or by other organizations. Internal means lie within the confines of the organization and include personnel and capital.

EXTERNAL MEANS

Certain organizations make use of nature; for example, nature provides lakes, oceans, rivers, and the air mass or space. Moreover, almost every organization makes use of certain facilities provided by society such as police and fire protection, roads, bridges, airports, and the post office. The majority of organizations also require the services provided by other firms. These include the facilities of middle-men (wholesalers, agents, and retailers), advertising agencies, newspapers, radio, television, insurance companies, banks, transportation firms, and a variety of public utility enterprises. These and many other external means are essential to the continued operation of many organizations. Also of great and often of more immediate importance to the management of organizations are the internal means of personnel and capital, the means that managers in an organization manage.

INTERNAL MEANS

The internal means of personnel and capital are the means over which the management of an organization has authority. The one that is the most difficult to manage is *personnel*. Although I do not wish to slight the importance or difficulty of managing *capital,* it is not as difficult as managing people. Why is this so? Since a piece of capital is an inanimate object or thing, it can be made to do precisely what we want it to do within the limits of its capacity. On the other hand, a person is highly intricate and complex. Each person possesses some similarities to others, but his many individual differences make his effective management no small undertaking. By proceeding from the most difficult to the least difficult of these two internal means, let us briefly examine the nature of personnel, which is of particular importance to administrators and managers in terms of their decisions.

To begin with, a human being is a biological or physiological organism. He responds to certain physical drives, including hunger and thirst, rest, sex, and elimination of waste. Moreover, the individual grows, ages, and experiences glandular changes, illnesses, and injuries. The physical condition of a person's body thus bears an important relationship to the efficiency of his work.

But man is much more than a physiological organism. He also has psychological characteristics. A man's personality is influenced by heredity and environment; his emotional make-up; his values, interests, attitudes, moods, and temperaments; his education; his experience; his habits and reflexes; his prejudices; and his intellect and will. Not only do these psychological characteristics exist in varying degrees, a fact which makes managing people a difficult task, but their influence upon a person's behavior also changes over time. Accordingly, a man who reports for work today is not the same man who reported for work yesterday.

Man is also a social animal. The influence of sociological factors such as culture, status, social class structure, and customs upon his behavior further complicates his being effectively managed. If we add up the physiological characteristics, the psychological characteristics, and sociological factors that affect the behavior of an individual on the job, it is easily seen that managing of capital is much less demanding than the effective managing of personnel. Nevertheless, the managers of any organization must make every effort to know as much as possible about the personal characteristics of their employees so that the administrators will be in the best position to make a sound choice of means whenever personnel is involved.

The other internal means of an organization are *capital means*. Inasmuch as the term "capital" has a variety of meanings, it seems appropriate to define the term for our purposes. Capital is defined as **all valuable objects of property used by the organization to carry on its operations.** The conception intended here is quite similar to the term *assets* as used by accountants. By "valuable objects of property" we mean intangible elements (patents, copyrights, franchises, securities, receivables, goodwill, etc.) as well as tangible or material elements (buildings, equipment, inventories, etc.).

Like personnel, capital also possesses certain characteristics of which managers should be aware. There are two characteristics of capital, (1) permanence, and (2) perishability. While these two characteristics of capital may initially seem to be contradictory, superficial analysis will quickly indicate that all capital is both permanent and perishable in a relative sense. All the items of capital mentioned in the preceding paragraph have varying degrees of permanence, from buildings to receivables, to cash. Yet each item is also perishable, through deterioration, as in the case of the depletion of soil fertility on agricultural land, or through change in value, as in the case of the effect of price-level fluctuations on cash and land.

It is important for managers to understand the two characteristics of capital because they frequently make decisions as to the choice of capital means, and they must constantly bear in mind the fact that although capital does possess degrees of permanence, its maintenance will have to be provided for by the management of any organization, since the use of the organization's capital as a means results in certain deterioration. Managers must not shy away from capital expenditures that provide for the replacement of the perishable elements of capital; otherwise the result may be the dangerous obsolescence of capital. Finally, the responsibility of attempting to keep the tendencies of capital toward perishability and permanence in some kind of *balance* must fall squarely upon the managers of any organization.

DEFINITION OF AN ORGANIZATION

After the discussion of goals and means, we are in a position to define the term "organization." **An organization is a complement of personnel and capital joined together in such a way as to efficiently perform certain well defined functions in order to effectively achieve certain clear-cut goals.** The various ways that personnel and capital may be joined together must wait for further study in a later chapter. At this point, however, it is appropriate to indicate the significance of goals and means to an organization. The definition points out that an organization exists to achieve goals through the engagement of the means of personnel and capital in well defined functions or activities.

Discussion Questions

1. What does the term "organization" mean to you? What is the formal definition of an organization?
2. Name some of the major forms of organizations. Classify them by legal form.
3. What is a goal? What are its synonyms? What are the major types of goals?
4. Define the term "means." What are the major types of means?
5. What role does the philosopher play with respect to goals and means?
6. What is an ultimate goal? What is your understanding of the following kinds of ultimate goals:
    (a) Financial goal
    (b) Employment goal
    (c) Return-to-labor goal
    (d) Production goal
7. Distinguish among the following terms: profit, net profit, pure profit, normal profit, profit-mongering.
8. Comment on the following statement: "Excessive profits are not characteristic of organizations in the United States."
9. Do nonprofit organizations earn income? If your answer is

yes, then how do nonprofit organizations differ from profit organizations?

10. What is the meaning of the phrase "excess of expense over income"?

11. Support or attack the thesis that employment should be a goal of organizations.

12. What is a "living wage"? Is a living wage unequivocal or without conditions?

13. Discuss the types of personal satisfactions that a person might expect while at work in any organization.

14. Has society generally approved of management's treatment of its employees? Explain.

15. Is production a means or a goal? Support your answer.

16. List the operating functions and the managing functions of organizations. What are the goals of each function?

17. Distinguish between functional goals and immediate goals. What is meant by "multiple goals" and "suboptimization"?

18. What is a job? A task? A motion?

19. "The management of personnel is more difficult than the management of capital." Is this statement true? False? Why?

20. What are some of the characteristics of personnel? What are the characteristics of capital? Why should managers be aware of these characteristics?

References

Davis, Keith, "The Public Role of Management," *Evolving Concepts in Management: Proceedings of the 24th Annual Meeting,* Edwin Flippo, ed. (University Park, Pennsylvania: Academy of Management, 1965), pp. 3-9.

Drucker, Peter F., *Concept of the Corporation* (New York: John Day, 1946), Chapter 1.

Drucker, Peter F., *The Practice of Management* (New York: Harper, 1954), Chapters 1, 2, 3, 7.

Duddy, Edward A., and David A. Revzan, *Marketing* (New York: McGraw-Hill, 1947), Chapter 1.

Flippo, Edwin B., *Principles of Personnel Management* (New York: McGraw-Hill, 1961), Chapter 20.

Galbraith, John K., *The New Industrial State* (Boston: Houghton Mifflin, 1967), Chapters 1, 5, 28, 30, 35.

Hardwick, C. T., and B. F. Landuyt, *Administrative Strategy* (New York: Simmons-Boardman, 1961), Chapter 4.

Hayek, F. A., "The Corporation in a Democratic Society," *Management and Corporations, 1985,* Melvin Anshen and George L. Bach, ed. (New York: McGraw-Hill, 1960), pp. 99-100.

Johnson, Robert W., *Financial Management* (Boston: Allyn & Bacon, 1959), Chapter 1.

Jones, Manley Howe, *Executive Decision-Making* (Homewood: Irwin, 1957), Chapter 1.

Larson, John A., ed., *The Responsible Businessman,* Readings from Fortune (New York: Holt, 1966), Parts III, IV.

MacEachern, Malcolm T., *Hospital Organization and Management* (Chicago: Physician's Record Company, 1957), Chapter 2.

McGregor, Douglas, *The Human Side of Enterprise* (New York: McGraw-Hill, 1960), Parts I-III.

Martin, Leroy T., *Hospital Accounting,* 4th ed. (Chicago: Physician's Record Company, 1964), Chapter 1.

Maslow, A. H., "A Theory of Human Motivation," *Psychological Review,* Vol. 50, July 1943, pp. 370-396.

Maynard, Harold H., and Theodore N. Beckman, *Principles of Marketing,* 4th ed. (New York: Ronald, 1946), Chapter 1.

Miller, David W., and Martin K. Starr, *Executive Decisions and Operations Research* (Englewood Cliffs: Prentice-Hall, 1960), Chapter 3.

Morell, R. W., *Managerial Decision-Making* (Milwaukee: Bruce, 1960), Chapter 2.

O'Donnell, Cyril, *et al., The Strategy of Corporate Research, A Symposium* (San Francisco: Chandler, 1967); see p. 190ff. of "The Strategy of Corporate Research and Development" by R. E. Gibson.

Robinson, Claude, *Understanding Profits* (Princeton: D. Van Nostrand Company, 1961), Chapters 1, 2, 13.

Simon, Herbert A., *Administrative Behavior* (New York: Macmillan, 1954), Chapter 1.

Smith, C. Aubrey, and Jim G. Ashburne, *Financial and Admin-*

istrative Accounting, 2nd ed. (New York: McGraw-Hill, 1960), Chapter 1.

Suojanen, Waino, *The Dynamics of Management* (New York: Holt, 1966), Chapters 7, 10, 12.

Walton, Clarence C., *Corporate Social Responsibilities* (Belmont: Wadsworth, 1967), Chapter 5.

Westing, J. H., I. V. Fine, and Members of the Milwaukee Association of Purchasing Agents, *Industrial Purchasing* (New York: Wiley, 1955), Chapter 1.

Weston, J. Fred, *Managerial Finance* (New York: Holt, 1962), Chapter 1.

Chapter 3. The Environment of Organizations

....

Environmental Influences
    The Ethical-Ideological Environment
    The Political-Legal Environment
    The Economic Environment
        The Market
        General Economic Conditions
        The Industry
        The Firm
    The Social Environment
    The Psychological Environment
    The Physical-Technological Environment

Conclusions

Appendix. Selected United States Government Publications

Discussion Questions

References

Chapter 3

The Environment of Organizations

Ideals are the world's masters.—J. G. HOLLAND

....

In the preceding chapter I outlined at length the goals and means of organizations. I presented a discussion of what is known as a *hierarchy of goals* or a *means-ends chain,* in which the lower order goals—immediate goals—become means of achieving the next higher order goals—intermediate goals—which in turn become a means of achieving the highest order of goals—the ultimate goals. To achieve any goal at any level, it is necessary to employ personnel and capital effectively.

The important thing to keep in mind about the choice and the achievement of goals is that they are never decided upon or achieved in a vacuum. On the contrary, the complex environment in which an organization operates requires that goals and means be carefully chosen with an acute awareness of the environment within which they shall have to be achieved. There is little doubt that organizations of earlier ages—whether in the Rome of the Caesars, the Baltic city of Lubeck, the "golden" city of Venice, Elizabethan England, or the Spain of Ferdinand and Isabella— were confronted with the problems of choosing and achieving goals within some environment. But the setting has changed for their twentieth century counterparts: the degree of problem complexity has increased almost geometrically; the political and legal restrictions have burgeoned out into areas previously untouched, workers have generally acquired greater bargaining power in their associations with employers, and customers individually and as members of dynamic social groups now require considerably more attention. In addition, the economic habitat of a capitalistic system, the psychological characteristics of members of organizations, and the highly complicated physical and technological environment within which a present-day organization must operate, all exert an appreciable influence upon the organization. Thus, an examination into the environment of organizations is essential, not only because of the paramount importance that any organization be aware of the environment within which its goals must be achieved, but also because of the necessity of adjusting the activities of any organization to the demands of a constantly changing environment.

ENVIRONMENTAL INFLUENCES

The alert manager of any organization should study the environment surrounding his organization to understand as fully as possible the forces at work *within* his organization as well as those *outside* his organization. The general climate in which the organization must achieve its goals is so important that some organizations employ psychologists, statisticians, economists, lawyers, sociologists, engineers, chemists, and others in an attempt to help managers understand the environment and potential changes in it. Managers, through their own efforts or with help, should try to anticipate future developments in their organization's environment. To assure that such effort is appropriately expended, managers must view the environment of their organizations in proper perspective. But the environment of an organization is so complex that it is impossible to analyze it as a whole. Consequently, the total environment must be subdivided so that it may be studied adequately. It should be understood at the outset, however, that the environment of an organization does not impinge itself upon the organization or come to managers in the neat, clear-cut packages described in this chapter. Even so, we shall attempt to understand the whole environment by discussing its six important parts: the ethical-ideological, the social, the political-legal, the economic, the phychological, and the physical-technological. The first type of environmental influence that we shall now examine is the *ethical-ideological* environment.

The Ethical-Ideological Environment

The terms "ethics" and "ideology" may quickly bring to the reader's mind thoughts about religion, morality, values, and perhaps even the conflict between the Western nations and the

Communist Bloc countries. It is less likely, however, that these terms will conjure up thoughts about organizations, particularly profit-making organizations. Although many organizations cannot be expected to function as a church or a family, ethical, moral, spiritual, philosophical, and idealistic values cannot be ignored by managers. Nor will it suffice to state that such considerations are too subjective for managers to deal with and that they ought to be left to clergymen and philosophers. While judgments about right or wrong, good or bad, moral or immoral are value judgments based upon value structures, which in turn are based upon the varying backgrounds and accumulated experiences of the individuals and groups concerned, it should be kept in mind that such judgments largely determine the kind of society we are to have, and consequently the kind of environment within which organizations must operate. Thus, in the real and actual world of industry, labor, management, business, nonprofit institutions, and the professions and government, there is an ethical-ideological dimension that cannot be ignored.[1]

A general view of history shows that the world has always been involved in varying degrees of ideological controversy. For example, in the fall of the Roman Empire, the Reformation, or the current upheaval between the West and the East, history reveals that men have aspirations and create and modify institutions in an attempt to realize their ideas. While most people have neither the interest nor the ability to create new ideas, their lives are nevertheless affected by many ideas of the thinkers and writers throughout history though often they are unaware of it. This is partly explained by the fact that ideas disseminate very slowly from the intellectuals and leaders to the masses. It may take decades, generations, or even centuries for some new ideas to eventually seep down to the people. The ideas of Aristotle, St. Thomas Aquinas, Martin Luther, Adam Smith, Karl Marx, Charles Darwin, Sigmund Freud, the Popes, John Dewey, William James, John Maynard Keynes, Frederick Taylor, Frank Gilbreth, and many more, for example, have been adopted by millions of people, many of whom lived long after them.

If management is to adequately adjust to its environment, it

---

[1] John A. Larson, ed., *The Responsible Businessman*, Readings from Fortune (New York: Holt, 1966), p. 262 of Louis Finkelstein's "The Businessman's Moral Failure."

must realize the importance of the ideas and aspirations of the people. The people, in response to their own ideas and the desire for fulfillment of their ideas, create and modify institutions, such as governments at all levels from local to world organizations, schools at all levels, churches, business organizations and non-profit organizations. If people believe that an organization is detrimental to them or to their ideas, they will set out to change that organization through various means, such as through their vote and their representatives in the government. As an example, we can look at the significant changes that have taken place in the present century in the United States with respect to certain groups like the labor unions, the farmers, the consumers, and the government agencies with which many organizations must deal.

It seems then that an organization must attempt to adapt itself to its ethical-ideological environment by choosing those goals and means which would make its conduct agree with the standards demanded by its environment. Since the Western world is largely based upon the Judaeo-Christian tradition and its moral and ethical principles, it is an exhilarating experience to realize that more and more managers engaged in the materialistic world of the market place are becoming deeply involved in the moral issues facing their organizations.[2] This does not mean, however, that we have a uniform code of ethics. It does mean that many professional and commercial organizations have developed codes of ethics intended to regulate the conduct of their members. In this connection, in recent years there has been a tendency to set up high level requirements and to develop detailed provisions. This trend has been fostered in the United States by the Federal Trade Commission (FTC) which has a department devoted exclusively to giving advice to business in the competitive fields and to help in the drafting of ethical codes.

In contemplating the ethical-ideological environment to which his organization must adapt, a manager realizes very quickly that in the real world failure to comply with the requirements

---

[2] *Ibid.*, pp. 261-262, Louis Finkelstein points out that scholars need the help and participation of businessmen in an attempt to draw upon the wisdom not only of Christianity and Judaism but also of Islamism, Buddhism, Confucianism and other traditions in their concern for "responsibility" in decision-making.

of this environment inevitably brings about some reaction. It may be a friendly warning, a strike, a lawsuit, a new law or regulation, or even liquidation of the organization. Whereas a manager should never run the risk of being faced with a boycott by society, he should realize that ethics and justice can and should be instrumental in his daily decision-making. He should recognize that any managerial or organizational conduct that violates the principle of justice is unethical. The manager who is reluctant to accept this principle should bear in mind the fact that the ethical-ideological environment significantly influences the political-legal environment. The structure of society is built initially upon ideologies and ethics,[3] and secondly upon law. With this important relationship in mind, let us now turn to the political-legal environment.

The Political-Legal Environment

In the preceding section we saw that the ethical-ideological environment was largely concerned with the adjustment of the organization to the ideas of the people with respect to morals, values, and justice. These ethical-ideological matters significantly influence and frequently anticipate changes in the political-legal environment of an organization, which is comprised of political concepts, government institutions, and the legal system. In a democratic society such the one in the United States, many of the ideas advocated and adopted by political parties are reflections of ethical-ideological trends which are eventually enacted into law by legislatures. The question of the relationship of the state to organizations thus becomes a matter of considerable importance when it is realized that many managerial decisions are more or less continuously affected by actions of the government.

In a democratic system of government, the relationship between the state and the organizations within the system is based upon the dual principles of private property and free enterprise.

[3] *Ibid.* Sidney Hook states on pp. 45 and 52 in his article "Bread, Freedom, and Businessmen" that fundamental economic decisions are moral choices which carry "responsibility" and "consequences" with them. Thus, one might easily infer from Hook's view, and the statement above that any managerial conduct that violates justice is unethical, that unethical decisions may well be irresponsible decisions. Such decisions may not only be detrimental to the organization but also to society.

The right of private property is the right to use, enjoy, dispose of, or otherwise exercise control over economic goods,[4] and free enterprise is a system in which economic activities are regulated largely through competition, but in which government has important responsibilities for making it work.[5] Since the early history of the laws governing property, property has been thought of as something which gives the owner an exclusive right to its use and enjoyment. Actually, there are important reservations on the rights of private property. These include the obligation to use property without curtailing the rights of other property owners, taxation, eminent domain, and the police power. Eminent domain is the right of the government to buy private property for public use; the police power of the state refers to those regulations, such as realty zoning laws, which safeguard the public health, morals, safety, and promote the general welfare. Similarly, the concept of free enterprise contains an important reservation. While a free enterprise system is based upon freedom of entry and exit into and out of organizations and occupations, equal opportunity among individuals often does not actually exist. For example, the heirs of men such as Cornelius Vanderbilt, John D. Rockefeller, Henry Ford, and Andrew Carnegie have a considerably greater opportunity, from the point of view of capital, to initiate some form of business enterprise than the young man who was born a pauper on the wrong side of the tracks. Nevertheless, even though strictly equal opportunity may not exist in many cases, there is unquestionably greater opportunity in the United States for the possible demonstration of leadership abilities by individuals without regard to race, color, or creed than in any other country on earth.

Free entry of organizations into industry gives rise to what is known as competition—a striving for rewards by two or more individuals or organizations. The term competition itself means a struggle, a contest, a rivalry. As long as managers of organiza-

[4] For a more complete and technical discussion of property, see any standard textbook on business law such as Ronald A. Anderson and Walter A. Kumpf, *Business Law*, 7th ed. (Cincinnati: South-Western, 1964), Chapter 4.

[5] See Part Two of Robert N. Corley and Robert L. Black, Jr., *The Legal Environment of Business* (New York: McGraw-Hill, 1963) for a complete discussion of the regulation of commerce and competition, taxation, and business and labor.

tions feel that they are partners in a community respecting the interests of society, they will compete fairly. If managers prefer not to participate in this partnership, they may risk indulgence in defamation, bribery, deception, and even violence. Indeed, the many limitations of human nature are constantly seen in competition within and among organizations. If the state looked the other way, some form of organizational civil war would perhaps take place. Consequently, it is obvious that wherever there is freedom of enterprise with competition some rules or laws for operation have to be established. Here the *principle of subsidiarity*[6] should prevail. The word *subsidiarity* stems from the Latin *subsidium* which means aid or assistance; that is, there should be as much responsible freedom as possible on the part of individuals and groups. There should only be as much law and government intervention in the lives of the people as is necessary to promote the common good of society. Moreover, the federal government should not perform those acts that can be performed adequately by the state government, nor should the state government perform what can be carried out adequately by local governments. Within the framework of the principle of subsidiarity, the state should attempt to prevent the misuse of freedom and maintain the efficiency of the competitive system. This would include the regulation of monopoly power and other means used to lessen competition, along with provisions to enable the state to meet emergencies. It should now be clear to the reader why, in addition to the entire body of statutory and common law making up the legal framework within which organizations must operate, we have laws regulating the behavior of competing organizations, such as the Sherman Anti-Trust Act, the Clayton Act, and the Robinson-Patman Act, and acts concerned with the relationship of management and labor, such as the Wagner Act and the Taft-Hartley Act.

Since organizations must be protected against other organizations and against the state, and since society must be protected against all organizations, managers can expect changes within the political-legal environment to be slow or rapid, depending upon the situation demanding action. The state may be com-

[6] Bernard W. Dempsey, *The Functional Economy* (Englewood Cliffs: Prentice-Hall, 1958), pp. 281-284.

pelled to act with speed and vigor in times of crisis. In times of less urgency, the rules and laws of the state may evolve slowly. In either case, management must adjust to this changing environment or expect to suffer whatever penalty is imposed for violation. Consequently, management should assume the responsibility of constraining government intervention in its affairs to a minimum by conducting its business on the basis of an enlightened self-interest for the benefit of the common good of society, while at the same time realizing a satisfactory achievement of the organization's goals. This may be done, for example, by means of associations of organizations within the trade or industry and/or by chambers of commerce attempting to privately eliminate difficulties that may arise, such as unfair competitive practices. Issues which cannot be resolved by private means will call for public means, and will then be submitted to the government for decision.

The Economic Environment

In the above discussion of the political-legal environment we saw that the concept of free enterprise gave rise to competition among organizations. Originating from the political-legal environment, competition also enters the economic environment as a most powerful factor forcing organizations to act quickly and efficiently in order to meet the requirements of economic survival. The existence of competition, plus the responsibility of the government to make a free enterprise system work, discloses the close relationship between the political-legal environment and the economic environment. This relationship is so intimate that the term *political economy* has often been used as a synonym for economics, especially in Europe.

Although the subject of economics is very broad and is variously defined, these matters need not concern us here since we are making no attempt to give a comprehensive treatment. Our purpose is to select some of the major economic factors that significantly affect organizations as they operate as going concerns, so that the reader may appreciate not only the complexity of the economic environment but also the pressing task facing managers as they make decisions in an attempt to adapt to this environment.

THE MARKET

One of the most important economic factors affecting organizations is the *market*. Here the organization meets its competitors, its customers, its suppliers: in short, anyone connected with the operations of the enterprise. Competition takes place in the market, where the struggle to win the customer is going on. It may be an urban market, a rural market, a highly organized market, an oligopolistic market (few producers or sellers), a wholesale market, a retail market, a cash market, a buying market, a selling market, and so on. The economic survival of an organization, especially in the long run, depends upon how well managers keep close watch and contact with market conditions. If an organization knows its market, both present and potential, it will be able to compete effectively within that market and even to expand its share, with a resulting increased sales volume.

The importance of the market in planning for the future can hardly be overestimated. The analysis of market factors as they affect the future involves what is known as forecasting. **"A forecast is a prediction or estimate of any future event or situation."**[7] As such, market forecasts range all the way from hunches or guesses by managers to such sophisticated techniques as correlation analysis, in which a relationship is discovered between or among the variables concerned. Forecasting is often viewed as a process that proceeds from the general to the specific. Thus forecasting may begin with general business or economic conditions, continue into an analysis of the industry, and end with a forecast for the particular organization. This procedure can admirably serve our needs here as we probe further into the economic environment. Let us then turn to the subject of general economic conditions.

GENERAL ECONOMIC CONDITIONS

A scientific search for reliable market information begins naturally with an inquiry into general economic or business conditions. Changes in economic conditions may not only affect the markets in which an organization buys and sells, but may also

[7] Frank D. Newbury, *Business Forecasting* (New York: McGraw-Hill, 1952), p. 4.

have an important effect on the optimism or pessimism of managers, as well as the general public, about the future of the national economy. Managers who have experienced a major depression do not easily forget it. Such an experience, in part at least, may be a reason why some of these managers have become conservative, perhaps even ultraconservative, and are very concerned and even preoccupied with the possibility of another depression. One need only recall the depression philosophy held by the late Sewell Avery of Montgomery Ward and Company after World War II. As the managers of this large mail-order house maintained excessive liquidity (especially cash) in the organization's assets instead of participating in the postwar expansion, its main competitor, Sears, Roebuck and Company, opened new stores and expanded as fast as possible.[8] As a result, Sears increased its sales and profits and captured a much greater share of the market in this industry.

While a knowledge of general business conditions may not always be of direct value to an organization, few matters seem to concern the manager more than the general state of the economy. Since the Great Depression of the thirties a great deal of attention has been given to the so-called *business cycle,* and businessmen have occupied themselves with the observation and interpretation of its movements. Indeed, perhaps more has been written about the business cycle than any other type of business variation.[9] Yet the economy does experience other kinds of variations: the *secular trend* is a much longer-term movement than the business cycle, whereas *seasonal fluctuations* are of much shorter duration. These variations may be envisioned as superimposed upon one another in Figure 3-1.

A secular trend reflects fundamental forces at work in the economy, such as the expansion in production of 2 to 3 per cent

---

[8] Sears made early use of the so-called "lease-back" arrangement. By this means, Sears would sell its store building to an insurance company looking for investment opportunities, then lease it back and pay a rental. This arrangement would thus free a great deal of capital for investment in increased inventories necessary to the expansion program.

[9] For a technical discussion of the business cycle, see Gottfried Haberler, *Prosperity and Depression,* 3rd ed. (Lake Success, N.Y.: United Nations, 1946) ; Alvin H. Hansen, *Business Cycles and National Income* (New York: Norton, 1951) ; and Robert M. Biggs, *National-Income Analysis and Forecasting* (New York: Norton, 1956) .

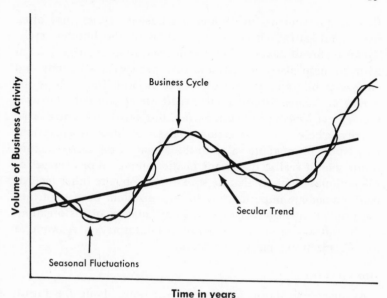

FIGURE 3-1. **Business fluctuations.**

per year or more for more than a half century in the United States. At the other extreme, seasonal fluctuations reflect, for example, weather conditions, vacations, and the Christian Christmas and Easter seasons. Business cycles fall somewhere in between seasonal fluctuations and secular trends. Some authorities have suggested that business cycles last somewhere from 3 to 12 years, although the time of the business cycle is difficult to establish because of the great many variables in the economy and the difficulties of precisely predicting their influence. Such variables as the level of inventories; demand; production; income; anticipated and actual expenditures for plant and equipment; employment; unemployment; population changes; the spending programs of the federal, state, and local governments; and business confidence, have an important effect upon the business cycle. Moreover, the increasing significance of the fiscal policy[10] (spending and taxa-

[10] In addition to fiscal policy, governments also engage in monetary policy (open market operations, discount rate and reserve requirement changes) and debt management (use of short- and long-term securities and varying

tion by governments to counter the business cycle) may often have a mitigating effect on vacillations of the business cycle. To keep abreast of general economic conditions, managers, often with the help of economists and/or other specialists, study and analyze public and private sources of information such as the *Survey of Current Business,* the *Wall Street Journal, Barron's,* the *Federal Reserve Bulletin, Forbes, Business Week,* and others. Finally, whereas a cross-section analysis of business conditions may be of considerable value to the manager, the alert administrator should realize that many of the summaries or averages of the national economy that he studies may obscure other facts of more immediate importance to his organization. Because of this, the prudent manager turns next to an analysis of his organization's industry or trade for additional information relevant to his organization's market situation.

THE INDUSTRY

As suggested above, forecasts or decisions about the future conditions of the market facing an organization require that managers look quite carefully at the firm's industry, as well as at the summaries or averages of the level of economic activity in all industries. This information is of considerable value, not only because it will acquaint an organization with its immediate competitors, but also because it will help to disclose an industry's position in relation to the nation's total business, and whether or not the industry is expanding or declining. In this connection, historical information about an industry, its capacity, the size and number of its competitors, its internal economic tendencies and changes in production and selling methods, and the prediction of conditions within the industry are very important matters to any dynamic organization. The automobile industry is a good example. Companies' shares of the market change even in such a rigid industry structure. The remarkable expansion of American Motors' share of the market up to 1965, in which a decline was experienced, along with the significant decline and rise in

---

maturities of debt) in their counter-cyclical policy actions. See Andrew F. Brimmer's "Initiative and Innovation in Central Banking," in *Business Topics,* Vol. 15, No. 3, Summer, 1967, pp. 7-15, for a comprehensive discussion of such public policy actions.

Chrysler's share of the market, indicates that important changes in an organization's position do take place even in such an oligopolistic industry. Hence, managers need to study industry information and patterns as well as general business conditions.

There are a number of sources of relevant information about an industry. There are *trade associations,* such as the Automobile Manufacturer's Association, which often prepare industry studies for the use of their members. *Professional associations* such as the Academy of Management, the American Economic Association, the American Marketing Association, the American Finance Association, and the American Accounting Association publish useful articles in their journals. *Government reports*[11] are available in a number of specific areas such as wholesaling, retailing, housing, and manufacturing. Useful information is also available at various *conventions and conferences* sponsored by different industry groups or organizations. Finally, the recent concept of "gamesmanship"[12]—reciprocal thinking or strategy as developed and played by some managers in an organization—is an attempt to anticipate competitors' moves in reaction decisions based upon original decisions made by the managers concerned in the "game." While this "game" usually begins with certain given data, additional information is frequently discovered or gleaned as a result of engaging in the process.

THE FIRM

With information about general economic conditions and the organization's industry, the manager now turns to the analysis of market factors that concerns his organization. The point of departure here is usually the development of the *revenue or sales forecast.* Internal factors, such as the organization's sales history, price policies, financial condition, costs, plant capacity, and planned promotional efforts, and the external factors discussed

[11] An alphabetical directory of United States Government periodicals and subscription publications can be found in the *Monthly Catalog* of United States Government publications, issued by the Superintendent of Documents, Washington, D.C. Selections from this comprehensive catalog will be found in the Appendix to this chapter as an indication of relevance and the breadth of coverage of government publications.

[12] For a more complete discussion of "gamesmanship" see C. T. Hardwick and B. F. Landuyt, *Administrative Strategy and Decision Making,* 2nd ed. (Cincinnati: South-Western, 1966), Chapter 1.

in the analysis of general economic conditions, become very important at this stage. Once the revenue or sales forecast is prepared by some appropriate method,[13] the organization, if it is a manufacturing firm, can prepare the *production forecast*. This forecast should specify the quantity and timing of production requirements along with the cost of materials, labor, and overhead. The *financial, administrative, and distribution expense forecasts* can now be prepared for the organization. With the foregoing forecasts in hand, the manager should now be in a more advantageous position to meet his competitors in the market place and to determine how well his organization is adapting to the economic environment.

The Social Environment

Up to this point we have discussed the ethical-ideological, political-legal, and economic influences in an organization's environment. We must now consider the social and psychological influences as well as the physical-technological forces in a dynamic organizational environment. Since the economic market place is significantly affected by groups and group behavior, let us first look at the social environment.

To understand the social environment, one must be aware of groups and their characteristics. An examination of the composition of groups will uncover many important features useful to managers in adjusting their organization to its environment. For example, the population in the United States will increase to over 300 million by the year 2000, which will provide a much broader market base for many organizations. Even more important than the size of the population, however, is its *distribution*. In other words, where is the population? The movement of large numbers of people to suburban areas after World War II has caused some businessmen in the urban shopping districts great hardships, and for some survival has become impossible. At the same time, other

---

[13] See Newbury, *Business Forecasting*, Chapter 15, for a discussion of these methods. Briefly, these methods fall into two broad classes: (1) methods which depend upon the projection of past experience and (2) methods which try to determine the current and future spending plans of consumers. Also see Harry D. Wolfe's *Business Forecasting Methods* (New York: Holt, 1966) for a discussion of forecasting methods based on the thesis that good forecasting must begin with good forecasting tools.

managers starting businesses in the suburban shopping centers found that the losses experienced by urban businessmen were gains for those suburban enterpreneurs who quickly adapted to the changes in the population distribution.

So that the astute manager will make few errors in judgment about his organization's potential market, he should be aware of other characteristics of the population. For example, *sex and age distribution* is important. There is a larger percentage of elderly people in the United States because of advances in medicine, and they have many special needs and desires. Firms manufacturing materials to fill these needs can expect an increase in the demand for those materials, and can look forward to broader markets. At the same time, the increase in the birth rate will also open up new markets for firms manufacturing materials for children. The expected increase in college enrollment by the years 1980-2000 should certainly benefit many firms anticipating this trend. For instance, book publishers are already planning for this period of increased demand in their market. Some publishing firms have merged for economic and competitive reasons, many are developing new series of textbooks at the college level, and they are increasing their advertising budgets. Yet it is interesting to note that some of the less dynamic publishing firms are not moving in these directions, indicating very slow adaptation to the changing environment within which they must operate.

Managers sometimes overlook group characteristics such as racial origins, occupations, living conditions, habits, social class and status seeking, and education.

Even superficial observation of our society quickly shows that people of different ethnic groups have different consumption patterns. Organizations serving Negroes are aware that the major Negro markets in the United States would include such metropolitan areas as New York City, Chicago, Philadelphia, Detroit, Washington, D.C., Los Angeles, and Baltimore. The French-American and Italian-American have helped many wine companies to flourish in this country, as well as processors of spaghetti, macaroni, and related products.

The *occupations, living conditions, and habits* of individuals can give managers information about markets. It would be unwise to open an exclusive and expensive restaurant with a lavishly furnished cocktail lounge in a rural community where most of the people are farmers, and more concerned with consumption of substantial portions of plain food at reasonable prices. As another example, though truck drivers in a large urban area may earn as much as lawyers, managers, or accountants, their respective spending patterns would likely be quite different. Therefore, if an organization is serving the needs of professional groups, managers should be aware of those needs and potential changes in their living conditions and in their habit patterns. While living conditions and habits of groups change slowly, they do change and can be an important influence upon market conditions.

An analysis of social environment cannot exclude *education, social class,* and *status seeking.* The dream of a classless society is indeed only a dream. One need only look around the community in which he lives to quickly discover that its social structure includes many classes.[14] While there are many ways to look at social strata, one approach is to envision it as a vertical continuum broken in half by a line (AB) separating the higher educated classes from the supporting classes (see Figure 3-2).

While vertical movement from lower to higher classes (from D toward C) on the scale is made with varying degrees of difficulty, any movement across the horizontal line (AB) is becoming quite rare and in the future will likely become very rare. I am acquainted with a number of large companies in urban areas that do not hire people without a college degree for the upper strata of management positions. Moreover, in some companies a college degree is essential for admittance to the company's management training programs. The days of Horatio Alger are quickly coming to an end in the United States. When an individual cannot advance in an organization because of lack of a college degree, or when he feels he is not advancing fast enough, he may try to feel superior in other ways. This is described as *status seeking*—the purchase and display of material possessions, civic and club par-

[14] It should be kept in mind in this discussion of social strata that different communities are not identical; that sociologists, social philosophers, social critics, and other social observers are entitled to have differences of opinion; and that I am making no attempt to be comprehensive; my purpose is merely to be indicative.

ticipation, standards of dress, and a degree of aloofness. It explains why many families needlessly have two or three cars, belong to the "right" clubs even though they can't afford it, wear expensive clothes, frequently bought on credit, from only prestige stores, and walk in a dignified manner in an attempt to convey the qualities of reservation and aloofness.

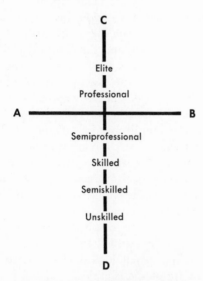

FIGURE 3-2. **A social-strata continuum.**

Elite: the wealthy and the high-prestige fashionable professionals.
Professional: all the other successful professionals and businessmen.
Semiprofessional: office workers, salesmen, technicians, nongraduate engineers, bookkeepers.
Skilled: mechanics, barbers, carpenters, skilled factory workers, linemen, bartenders, stenographers.
Semiskilled: factory operatives, truck drivers, clerks, machine operators, attendants, waitresses, riveters.
Unskilled: domestics, janitors, gardeners, laborers, street cleaners, miners, dishwashers.

What does all this mean to organizations? It means a bonanza of sales based upon the need for prestige, status, individuality, social decorum, emulation, dignity, and pride. *If an organization can make people feel superior if they buy its products, it is likely to have embarrassingly large profits.* Thus, all aspects of the social environment significantly affect the demand for goods and an organization's markets, so much so that a manager's lack of attention to the changes in this environment could be serious, or even disastrous.

The Psychological Environment

The preceding section was concerned with groups and their characteristics. But groups are made up of men. And men are the most important elements *within* any organization as well as *outside* the organization. The men within the organization are the investors, the managers, and the employees; the men outside the organization are the customers and the suppliers. Dealing with people can be called the essence of management and, to a great extent, is the manager's primary and most difficult job. The administrator should know that every individual is different and that his responses to stimuli may be different. Accordingly, since men and their actions are of paramount importance to organizations, it is necessary for managers to attempt to understand something of man's psychological characteristics. To attempt a thorough study of human nature would, of course, be an undertaking far too pretentious for our purpose because it would require a careful search of the sciences of physiology and psychology. Rather, we shall have to be satisfied with a cursory examination of some of man's major psychological characteristics so that the reader will be aware of the complexity of the psychological environment, and, consequently, aware of the manager's need for some knowledge of psychology so that he can adapt to this important segment of an organization's environment.

As was discussed in Chapter 2, a human being is a complex, *physiological structure*. The structure has many parts, but includes principally the muscular system, the digestive system, the respiratory system, the circulatory system, the skeletal system, the nervous system, and the genito-uruinary system.[15]

A human being also inherits certain physical and psychological characteristics from his parents. When we look at *physical structure, heredity,* and the effects of an individual's *environment,*

[15] See E. M. Greisheimer, *Physiology and Anatomy*, 7th ed. (Philadelphia: Lippincott, 1955), Units II-V, for a detailed analysis of these systems.

education, and *experience,* we can begin to see why people differ in their values, prejudices, attitudes, temperaments, habits, reflexes, and learned responses. Individuals are also affected in varying degrees by their *emotions* as they respond to situations in their private or organizational life. Some people have developed considerable emotional control, while others seem to be controlled largely by their emotions. In addition, the individual is endowed with an *intellect* and a *will.* The intellect permits the individual to engage in the highest form of activity known among animals—reasoning. Although it seems that most human actions proceed from emotion rather than from reason, nevertheless man's intellect permits him to use facts and concepts in an attempt to solve a problem not adequately solvable by other means such as impulse, reflex, or habit. The intellect, after deliberation, presents reasonable solutions to the will for acceptance or rejection. The power of the will and the need for training the will become clear when we realize that an individual is capable of deciding against reason if he wills.[16]

The foregoing paragraphs present some idea of man's psychological make-up. First, man is a physiological organism, whose emotions, values, reason, and volition or will are influenced by environment, education, and experience.[17] These characteristics make man's effective management quite difficult, because they exist in varying degrees. Also, their effects change within each individual over a period of time. Nonetheless, an organization must operate and must attempt to manage itself with the psychological environment as its primary concern. To operate otherwise could lead to low morale and higher costs, and, in the final stages of mismanagement, even to liquidation of the firm.

[16] See Francis L. Harmon, *Principles of Psychology,* rev. ed. (Milwaukee: Bruce, 1951) , Chapter 4 for a technical discussion of the causes of individual differences. In addition, if the reader is inclined to delve further into the nature of volition or will, he may consult with considerable gain the English translations of the following classic works of the German scholar, Johannes Lindworsky: *The Training of the Will,* translated by Steiner & Fitzpatrick (Milwaukee: Bruce, 1932) and *The Psychology of Asceticism,* translated by Emil A. Heiring (Baltimore: Carroll, 1950) .

[17] Refer to C. E. M. Joad, *How our Minds Work* (New York: Philosophical Library, 1955) for a complete discussion of the mind-body (mental-physical) interrelationship.

Far forward among management imperatives is an under-standing of motivation. And fortunately for the manager, the behavioral scientists have presented us with a number of possible approaches to motivation. The Maslow-McGregor analysis pre-sented in Chapter 2 is a case in point. But there are others. For example, there is the famous "Hawthorne effect" discovered by the late Elton Mayo and his associates from Harvard between 1927 and 1932 at the Hawthorne works of the Western Electric Company in Chicago. Mayo realized that employees' receiving unaccustomed attention had the effect of coalescing previously indifferent individuals into cohesive groups, thus making the group more conscious of itself, increasing group esprit de corps, and enhancing morale.[18] The result was that the workers de-voted themselves wholeheartedly to their work; in other words, they were motivated.

Other researchers have also addressed themselves to the prob-lem of motivation. Rensis Likert and Chris Argyris both take the point of view that the style of leadership—the supervisory style—must be appropriate to the employees' needs and the job require-ments rather than be production-centered or production-oriented, where the supervisor functions primarily as an autocrat. More-over, both Likert and Argyris feel that management control often becomes an end in itself, narrowing management's perspective, rather than a means to an end. Likert believes that management should permit some participation by employees so that they share information and some decision-making responsibility. Argyris advocates a deliberate attempt at flexibility in leadership styles and management controls and the strengthening of interpersonal processes through sensitivity training—a process in which per-sonnel are made aware of their personal impact on others, thereby reducing communication barriers.[19]

Finally, Daniel Katz and Robert L. Kahn have attempted to

[18] Saul W. Gellerman, *The Management of Human Relations* (New York: Holt, 1966), pp. 27-32. For a retrospective analysis see H. Landsberger's *Hawthorne Revisited* (Ithaca: Cornell University Press, 1958).

[19] *Ibid.*, Chapters 3 and 4. See also Rensis Likert, *New Patterns of Manage-ment* (New York: McGraw-Hill, 1961) and Chris Argyris, *Personality and Organization* (New York: Harper, 1957) for complete analyses of the Likert and Argyris theories.

classify motivational patterns in organizations under four major headings as in Figure 3-3.

A. *Legal compliance.* Securing acceptance of role prescriptions and organizational controls on the basis of their legitimacy. The rule enforcement approach of simple machine theory. Controlling production through the speed of the assembly line.

B. *The use of rewards or instrumental satisfactions for inducing required behaviors.* The approach of modified machine theory.

    (1) System rewards earned through membership or seniority in system such as fringe benefits, cost-of-living raises, or other benefits across the board.

    (2) Individual rewards such as pay incentives and promotion on the basis of individual merit.

    (3) Instrumental identification with organizational leaders in which followers are motivated to secure the approval of leaders.

    (4) Affiliation with peers to secure social approval from own group.

C. *Internalized pattern of self-determination and self-expression.* The satisfactions from accomplishment and the expressions of talents and abilities.

D. *Internalized values and the self-concept.* The incorporation of organizational goals or subgoals as reflecting values or self-concept.

FIGURE 3-3. **Motivational patterns for producing various types of required behaviors.** Source: Daniel Katz and Robert L. Kahn, *The Social Psychology of Organizations* (New York: Wiley, 1966), p. 341.

Type A uses the concept of legitimacy as postulated by the German economist, Max Weber, at the turn of the twentieth century. It is a concept that refers to situations in which widespread compliance occurs. In other words, many functionaries or administrators carried out the laws and policies of the organization—the bureaucracy. Type B includes the military concept of command. However, a second form of motivation is attempted here—the linking of certain rewards to desired behaviors. In Type A and Type B, individuals act because of organizational law; it is their duty to obey. On the other hand, in Types C and D, activities are rewarding in themselves. Motivation is internalized so that performance occurs without supervision. In Type C, satisfactions come from role performance—thus, the department head derives gratification from the exercise of his leadership skills. Type D goes even further, with the concept of internalized motivation, by which an individual is activated toward group goals because such goals are synonymous with his own value system. In Types C and D we can see the resemblance to the ego and self-fulfillment part of the Maslow-McGregor analysis in Chapter 2.

The Physical-Technological Environment

The physical-technological environment is concerned with natural and physical phenomena as well as with technological innovations or developments. The term "innovation" means **the introduction of new ideas and techniques that result in lower costs, higher production, or increased revenues.** The physical phenomena include the land, its topography, fertility, water supply, and vegetation; natural conditions such as climate, seasons, and temperature; and man-made modifications, such as buildings, roads, and drainage systems. In an industrial society, smoke, odors, and gases are included among the physical phenomena to which an organization may have to adjust. To some organizations involved in agriculture, mining, commercial fishing, construction, and transportation, the physical phenomena with which they must deal are obviously of major importance to them in their operations. To other firms not engaged in the extractive industries, construction, or transportation, the physical phenomena may be less important but still require careful consideration.

Although different firms will find that the physical phenomena that surround them are of varying importance to them, from the point of view of adaptation most firms should be quite concerned about competitors' technological improvements or innovations. The executive must attempt to keep pace with competitors' innovations if his organization is to survive and prosper. In this regard, the manager should be aware that many innovations take place in areas other than mechanics and engineering. Although the invention of the wheel, assembly line production, and automation have been innovations of major importance to the smooth functioning of an organization, of no less importance are the development of decentralized management, better organizational techniques, improved human relations approaches, better recruitment and selection procedures, more rational approaches to decision-making, advertising innovations, better financial arrangements for customers, refined accounting methods, and new marketing research tools. The goals of the research and development function defined in Chapter 2 take on real meaning in the physical-technological environment. The stress of competition and substitution compels organizational concern with research and development of new products, services, and processes. Moreover, managers should take whatever measures are necessary to prohibit disclosure of important innovations to competing companies. Technological improvements represent one way of competing in the market place. Consequently, security measures may be necessary for managers to protect an organization's trade secrets. Some unscrupulous competitors may leave no stone unturned to uncover the innovations of other firms. Some have even had recourse to various forms of espionage to achieve their ill-conceived goals.

CONCLUSIONS

The foregoing survey of the major environmental influences affecting the operations of any organization enables us to make a number of inferences. One, the goals of organizations cannot be effectively achieved unless organizations adjust their activities to environmental demands. Two, some factors within the total environment change slowly, while others are modified more quickly. Three, adaptation to an organization's environment requires (a) awareness of masses of data, information, and concepts about the environment and (b) a dynamic program for adapting to the ever-changing environment. Four, it is clear that managers need to know as much as possible about such fields as sociology, psychology, economics, political science, law, ethics, the physical sciences, and engineering to better understand the complicated environmental setting within which an organization must exist, operate, and adjust. Finally, moderate or relatively ineffectual adjustment by an organization to its environment will result in the expenditure of time and money to solve avoidable problems. In the extreme, voluntary or involuntary dissolution of the organization will eventually be the final result.

Appendix. Selected United States Government Publications

Area trends in employment and unemployment. Employment Security Bureau, Manpower Administration, Labor Department.

Assets and liabilities of all member banks by districts. Federal reserve statistical release, G.7.1; Federal Reserve System Board of Governors.

Bank debits and deposit turnover. Federal reserve statistical release key number G.6; Federal Reserve System Board of Governors.

Bureau of Census catalog. Census Bureau, Commerce Department.

Comptroller General decisions. General Accounting Office.

Construction review. Monthly industry report; Business and Defense Services Administration, Commerce Department.

Consumer credit. Federal reserve statistical release, G.19; Federal Reserve System Board of Governors.

Consumer price index. Labor Statistics Bureau, Labor Department.

Cost reduction journal. Directorate for Cost Reduction, Office of Assistant Secretary of Defense; Defense Department.

Current industrial reports. Census Bureau, Commerce Department.

Current population reports. Census Bureau, Commerce Department.

Current retail trade reports. Census Bureau, Commerce Department.

Digest of decisions of National Labor Relations Board. National Labor Relations Board.

Economic development. Economic Development Administration, Commerce Department.

Economic indicators. Economic Joint Committee, Congress.

Employment and earnings, and monthly report on labor force. Labor Statistics Bureau, Labor Department.

Factory labor turnover. Labor Statistics Bureau, Labor Department.

Federal reserve bulletin. Federal Reserve System Board of Governors.

Federal Trade Commission news summary. Federal Trade Commission.

Health, education, and welfare indicators. Office of Assistant Secretary for Program Coordination, Health, Education, and Welfare Department.

Hill-Burton project register. Division of Hospital and Medical Facilities, Public Health Services, Health, Education, and Welfare Department.

Interstate Commerce Commission decisions. Interstate Commerce Commission.

Marketing information guide, annotated bibliography. Business and Defense Services Administration, Commerce Department.

Monthly checklist of State publications. Exchange and Gift Division, Processing Department, Library of Congress.

Monthly department store sales by departments. Federal Reserve System Board of Governors.

Monthly labor review. Labor Statistics Bureau, Labor Department.

N.L.R.B. statistical summary. National Labor Relations Board.

National summary of business conditions. Federal Reserve System Board of Governors.

Occupational outlook quarterly. Labor Statistics Bureau; Labor Department.

Public management sources. Library, Budget Bureau, Executive Office of the President.

Quarterly financial report for manufacturing corporations. Federal Trade Commission.

Sales, profits, and dividends of large corporations. Federal Reserve System Board of Governors.

Social security bulletin. Social Security Administration, Health, Education, and Welfare Department.

Statistical bulletin. Securities and Exchange Commission.

Statistical reporter. Office of Statistical Standards, Budget Bureau, Executive Office of the President.

Survey of current business. Business Economics Office, Commerce Department.

Treasury bulletin. Treasury Department.

United States Government research and development reports. Clearinghouse for Federal Scientific and Technical Information, Institute for Applied Technology, National Bureau of Standards, Commerce Department.

Unemployment insurance review. Unemployment Insurance Service, Employment Security Bureau, Manpower Administration, Labor Department.

Unemployment insurance statistics. Employment Security Bureau, Manpower Administration, Labor Department.

Discussion Questions

1. "Goals of organizations are never achieved in a vacuum." What does this statement mean?
2. Name the important environmental influences facing managers. Why are they important?
3. "The ethical-ideological dimension of a firm's environment can be ignored with little or no loss to the organization." Is this statement true? False? Why?
4. What do the terms "ethics" and "ideology" mean to you?
5. What role can the Federal Trade Commission play with respect to the ethical-ideological environment?
6. When is managerial, business, or organizational conduct unethical?
7. What is meant by the concepts of "private property" and "free enterprise"? Do these principles mean that there is "equal opportunity" among individuals in the United States?
8. Define the following terms: competition, subsidiarity, enlightened self-interest, monopoly power, economics, political economy, oligopolistic market.
9. "One of the most important factors in the economy affecting organizations is the market." What are the implications of this statement?
10. What is a forecast? Name some forecasting methods. What is the purpose of a revenue forecast? What is the purpose of an expense forecast?
11. What is meant by a secular trend, the business cycle, and

seasonal fluctuations? What are some of the causes of these business variations?

12. Is the business cycle problem solved? What role do the government and the law play in this connection?
13. Why should managers know as much as possible about the industry of which their organization is a member? Name several growth industries and several declining industries.
14. What is meant by the concept of "gamesmanship"?
15. The size and distribution of the population is a significant factor to organizations. Why is this so?
16. "Consumption patterns of most people are essentially the same." Is this statement true? False? Explain.
17. Of what importance are *social class* and *status seeking* to certain organizations?
18. What are some of the causes of individual differences? Of what importance to management are these individual differences among people?
19. What "physical phenomena" are important to organizations in attempting to adjust to their environment? What are innovations? Name some major and some minor innovations of recent times.
20. In order to better understand the environment of his organization, the professional manager should not limit his knowledge to professional subjects such as management, marketing, accounting, and finance. In what other fields should managers attempt to ground themselves?

References

Albers, Henry H., *Organized Executive Action* (New York: Wiley, 1961), Chapter 11.

Anderson, Ronald A., and Walter A. Kumpf, *Business Law,* 5th ed. (Cincinnati: South-Western, 1956), Chapters 5, 13, 14.

Argyris, Chris, *Personality and Organization* (New York: Harper, 1957).

Biggs, Robert M., *National Income Analysis and Forecasting* (New York: Norton, 1956), Chapters 1, 11.

Brimmer, Andrew F., "Initiative and Innovation in Central Banking," *Business Topics,* Vol. 15, No. 3, Summer, 1967, pp. 7-15.

Corley, Robert N., and Robert L. Black, Jr., *The Legal Environment of Business* (New York: McGraw-Hill, 1963), Part 2.

Dempsey, Bernard W., *The Functional Economy* (Englewood Cliffs: Prentice-Hall, 1958), Chapters 11, 14-16, 19, 21.

Dimock, Marshall E., *A Philosophy of Administration* (New York: Harper, 1958), Chapter 7.

Gellerman, Saul W., *The Management of Human Relations* (New York: Holt, 1966), pp. 27-32.

Greisheimer, E. M., *Physiology and Anatomy,* 7th ed. (Philadelphia: Lippincott, 1955), Units II-V.

Haberler, Gottfried, *Prosperity and Depression,* 3rd ed. (Lake Success, N.Y.: United Nations, 1946), Chapters 2-6, 8-11.

Hansen, Alvin H., *Business Cycles and National Income* (New York: Norton, 1951), Parts 1, 2.

Hardwick, C. T., and B. F. Landuyt, *Administrative Strategy and Decision Making,* 2nd ed. (Cincinnati: South-Western, 1966), Chapter 1.

Harmon, Francis L., *Principles of Psychology,* rev. ed. (Milwaukee: Bruce, 1951), Chapters 4, 12, 16-18.

Jancaukas, Raymond C., "Gift Acceptance by Company Personnel," *Personnel Journal,* Vol. 40, No. 1, May, 1961, pp. 22-25.

Joad, C. E. M., *How our Minds Work* (New York: Philosophical Library, 1955).

Jones, Manley H., *Executive Decision-Making* (Homewood: Irwin, 1957), Chapters 10, 11.

Katz, Daniel, and Robert L. Kahn, *The Social Psychology of Organizations* (New York: Wiley, 1966), p. 341.

Landsberger, H., *Hawthorne Revisited* (Ithaca: Cornell University Press, 1958).

Larson, John A., ed., *The Responsible Businessman,* Readings from Fortune (New York: Holt, 1966).

Lassance, Ralph A., "Christianity and Social Progress," *Marquette Business Review,* Vol. VI, No. 1, Winter, 1962, pp. 26-36.

Likert, Rensis, *New Patterns of Management* (New York: McGraw-Hill, 1961).

Lindworsky, Johannes, *The Training of the Will,* translated by Steiner and Fitzpatrick (Milwaukee: Bruce, 1932).

Lindworsky, Johannes, *The Psychology of Ascetism,* translated by Emil A. Heiring (Baltimore: Carroll, 1950).

Morell, R. W., *Managerial Decision-Making* (Milwaukee: Bruce, 1960), Chapters 1, 2.

Newbury, Frank D., *Business Forecasting* (New York: McGraw-Hill, 1952), Chapters 1, 15.

Selekman, Benjamin M., *A Moral Philosophy of Management* (New York: McGraw-Hill, 1959), Chapters 8, 12, 16, 28.

The Spiritual and Moral Significance of Free Enterprise, A Symposium Presented at the 66th NAM Congress of American Industry (New York: National Association of Manufacturers, 1961), pp. 3-43.

Weimer, Arthur M., *Business Administration* (Homewood: Irwin, 1962), Chapters 4, 20-24.

Wolfe, Harry D., *Business Forecasting Methods* (New York: Holt, 1966), Chapters 1, 2.

Chapter 4. **The Nature of Management**

...

The Meaning of Management
Management and Administration
Management as a Science
Management as an Art

The Purpose of Management

The Theory of Management

The Methods of Management
Rule-of-Thumb Management
Management by Autocracy
Management by the Scientific Method
Facts or Data
Inferences
Models
Limitations
Management by Participation

The Functions of Organizations
The Operating Functions
Purchasing
Producing
Marketing
Financing
Accounting
Research and Development
Facilitating
The Functions of Management
Decision-Making: The Essence of Management
The Traditional Functions of Management
Relationship of Management Functions to Operating Functions

Discussion Questions

References

Chapter 4

The Nature of Management

Good management consists in showing *average* people
how to do the work of *superior* people.—JOHN D. ROCKEFELLER

■■■

THE MEANING OF MANAGEMENT

Management and Administration

Closely related to the term *management* is the term *administration*. Some writers insist upon maintaining a careful distinction between the two terms, some use them synonymously, and others refrain from giving attention to them at all. Although the dictionary meanings and business and industry usage increasingly indicate interchangeability between the two terms, there are still those who think of "administration" as referring to those activities or functions performed by executives who occupy the higher positions in organizations, especially large organizations. A distinction is thus made between the broad policy decisions made at the upper levels of the hierarchy and the somewhat less broad implementing or executing decisions made at middle or lower levels.

It seems to me that this distinction is one of degree rather than one of kind. Decision-making and management are general types of activity which do not vary according to organizational level. Rather, they are essentially the same process anywhere; the only thing that changes is the subject matter to which the process is applied. People at higher organizational levels may deal with broader, company-wide subject matter, while those at lower organizational levels deal with more narrow divisional, departmental, or subdepartmental matters. In either case, management or administration is the same kind of activity at any hierarchical level. There are differences in the scope of the impact of decisions at different levels, but no differences in the kinds of activities performed.

Others prefer to use the word "administration" because they feel that the term "management" has emotional overtones and too readily conjures up the unfortunate image of the labor-management dichotomy.[1] This choice of terminology really appears to be one of "desire" rather than one of "reason" because even if we assume that the term *management* carries the emotional connotations of labor-management problems, the term *administration* does not escape this characteristic. To many people, the term "administration" has a more lofty, brassy, and commanding ring which frequently casts an authoritative and somewhat negative reflection than does the more down-to-earth term of "management."

In many nonprofit organizations such as hospitals, educational institutions, and public corporations, the principal officers are more commonly referred to as "administrators" rather than "managers." Thus, we have executives more frequently referred to as hospital administrators, educational administrators, and government or public administrators rather than as managers in these public or quasipublic organizations. Such usage stems more from custom and habit than from any essential difference between the process of "administration" and the process of "management."

Finally, since the differentiation claimed by some between *management* and *administration* is largely the product of desire and tradition rather than any essential difference in the functions of the process of management or administration, for the purpose of our discussion the two terms "administration" and "management" will be considered synonymous and will be used interchangeably.

Management as a Science

Much has been written and spoken about the subject of management as a science. The question as to whether management is a science depends upon what we mean by a *science*. If we

---

[1] C. T. Hardwick and B. F. Landuyt, *Administrative Strategy and Decision Making,* 2nd ed., (Cincinnati: South-Western, 1966) , p. 4.

mean a branch of knowledge in the limited sense of the natural sciences, then management cannot be called a science, because in the natural sciences rigorous experimentation, in which phenomena are defined, analyzed, measured, varied, and repeated, enables the scientist to search for a proof. Because of the great many variables in dealing with people and with the future, and since it is impossible to control these variables strictly, similar experimentation is not possible in management. In management, where we are dealing with people, the circumstances vary considerably because of differences in personality, intelligence, environment, and the like. However, the fact that management is not an exact science does not inhibit managers from making use of the natural sciences. Managers frequently make use of chemistry, physics, geology, and engineering.

If we broaden our concept of science to mean any organized body of knowledge, management qualifies as a science with the other nonphysical sciences of philosophy, mathematics, medicine, politics, economics, psychology, and sociology. Management is thus considered to be a science in this sense, because it is an organized body of knowledge set forth in the form of principles or fundamental truths.

Of much more importance to management is whether or not managers are using scientific methods. Even though management is not a physical science, it is quite possible for managers to make use of scientific methods. This will be discussed at length in a later secton of this chapter.

Management as an Art

In the foregoing section we have established that management is a science because it is an organized body of knowledge. The next question is corollary: Is management an art? As with the term "science," the answer depends upon what we mean by *art*. If by "art" we mean only the fine arts such as music, painting, drama, and sculpture, management cannot be called an art. But if by art we mean the creative use of the application of principles to situations in order to achieve certain results, management qualifies as an art, since management must accomplish things through the application of principles developed out of experience.

The study of management in order to learn the principles of management is hardly half the battle. It seems to me utterly vain and useless to know the fundamental truths of management if we do not employ them for the end for which they were intended. This is the important point in studying and learning the principles of management. It is of little value to know the truths of management unless we intend to practice them.

THE PURPOSE OF MANAGEMENT

Although the foregoing statements about the meaning of management suggest the purpose of management, a brief summarizing statement at this point may be of value. Why is it necessary for managers to engage in management? In order to achieve the goals of the organization? Yes, but could not the goals of an organization be achieved without their guidance? Perhaps, ideally, some minimum level of goal realization could be achieved without the manager if all personnel were capable of effective self-management in the performance of their duties. Unfortunately, in reality we find that the employees' unsupervised performance does not assure the realization of an organization's goals, because many people are unable to perform their activities effectively without guidance and leadership. Moreover, they are frequently unable to relate their activities to those of others in the same organization. In other words, management is necessary in an organization because the people who perform the purchasing, producing, marketing, financing, accounting, research and development, and facilitating functions cannot *coordinate* all the activities necessary for the maximum attainment of goals unless their own activities are deliberately and efficiently managed. Moreover, even management itself must be managed, especially in large organizations, if an optimum achievement of an organization's goal is to be realized. This is the purpose of management which imposes a serious responsibility upon managers. This responsibility is so important that it cannot be delegated. Managers and only managers are ultimately responsible for coordinating activities so that the organization's goals and its successful operation may be realized.

THE THEORY OF MANAGEMENT

Earlier in this chapter we established that management is a science because it is an organized body of knowledge set forth in the form of principles as fundamental truths, and that it is an art in which principles are applied to problematic situations. Such principles form a conceptual framework or theory of management which can serve as guideposts for a manager's decisions and actions, thus minimizing errors. I should mention here that the word *theory* has at least two important meanings. One is **an unproved hypothesis which requires testing to establish its validity.** The other is **a generalization or principle which is based upon empirical research or experience**—the only sense in which the term "theory" is used in this book. To say that "an organized statement of the principles of management is the theory of management" is to mean that these principles are fundamental truths of management which have been tested in the industrial, business, and institutional world. Such empirical testing gives principles validity. If a pseudoprinciple or quasiprinciple does not stand up under empirical testing, it is rejected as a principle because it is not a fundamental truth. If a principle does withstand such testing, it is accepted as valid and may be justly classified as part of the theory of management. Thus, theory as tested principles or concepts of management is both practical and applicable.

Without principles of management it would not be possible to teach and train students in the theory of management for future managerial positions. While a college or university cannot train "finished" executives, it can give the student basic concepts with which to begin the management development process. With an orderly framework of management concepts plus some experience in solving management case problems through decision-making, the student is ready to enter the business and/or institutional world.

THE METHODS OF MANAGEMENT

Reference has already been made in this chapter to the use of scientific methods by managers. Before exploring this specific

methodology, it is relevant to consider some of the other management methods used by some managers. The reader will then
be in a position to compare these methods with the scientific
method and judge for himself which is the best for him to use.

Rule-of-Thumb Management

Rule-of-thumb management, sometimes called "off the cuff"
management, is that form of management in which some managers do largely what they *desire* to do. Very often this means
doing nothing, managing by default, or maintaining the *status
quo* until some crisis develops. When a crisis develops in which
little or no time is available for reflection, the rule-of-thumb
manager applies uncritically what he knows, what he has used
somewhere before, or simply what he desires to apply. This form
of management can be characterized as *subjective*. Thus, intuition, habits, emotions, impulses, fixations, reflexes, pretentions,
defenses, and caprice describe this approach to management. Of
course, not all decisions and actions of rule-of-thumb managers
must be assumed to be wrong or ineffective. On the contrary,
many of their decisions and actions may have good results. But
such outcomes are not usually because of the rule-of-thumb
method; rather, they are frequently in spite of this method.
As a matter of fact, the law of averages, the existence of chance
factors, and luck have just as much influence on a rule-of-thumb
manager as they do upon others who follow more rigorous methods of management. It is interesting to note in this connection
that the "mental revolution" in management thought since the
time of Frederick W. Taylor, which is displacing tradition and
rule-of-thumb management by more rational methods, is being
made against the determined opposition of the rule-of-thumbers,
who are convinced that what they do is right because they are
doing it and not because of evidence and/or rationality. Attacks by rule-of-thumbers against more rational processes of
management have always met with wide acclaim because they
strike a responsive note in human nature—take the road of least
resistance. While rule-of-thumb management may appear to give
some managers the feeling of subjective certainty, because of the
lack of reflective thought it actually reduces the probability of
desirable outcomes and increases the element of uncertainty in

management. Moreover, it can offer no objective proof that it is the best method of management or that other methods are erroneous.

Management by Autocracy

Perhaps the most primitive method of management is management by the autocrat. This is a somewhat tragic form of management because it is management by a dictator. The late Sewell Avery of Montgomery Ward and Company and the original Henry Ford ran their organizations for many years as virtual dictatorships. In this method of management, the employer arbitrarily forces his subordinates to accept his authority without question. The autocrat is a firm believer in the master-servant relationship as far as he and his employees are concerned. Consequently, the autocrat has very little concern for the dignity of man or for the welfare of employees on or off the job. Laborers are regarded as just another factor of production much like land and capital, to be dealt with as a necessary evil rather than as human beings with emotions, desires, needs, hopes, and goals of their own. Such an employer or manager is stern and aloof, bluffs, uses negative motivation such as fear of penalties, discharges employees rapidly, and tends to discipline personnel in public rather than in private. Actually, the approach of the autocrat appears to be a defense mechanism because of a basic feeling of insecurity, inferiority, and incompetence. He feels that his appearance as a tough guy skillfully conceals his doubts, his feelings of uncertainty, and his state of indecision. The art of understanding, appreciating, respecting and being considerate of people is not for him. He would rather be a lonely ego-maniac who is the boss and who wants everyone to know it and never forget it. It is an understatement to say that such a manager is less than inspiring. However, there is one comforting observation about the autocrat—he appears less frequently as professionally trained managers slowly but surely move into positions of authority in the United States.

Management by the Scientific Method

As mentioned in the discussion of rule-of-thumb management, Frederick W. Taylor pioneered the scientific method of management around the beginning of the twentieth century. He insisted at that time, and rightly so, that scientific management is a method of approaching management problems. Let us look at the essential characteristics of this method.

FACTS OR DATA

The scientific method requires the use of facts or data. **Facts or data are phenomena existing in the real world that are observed and known through the senses.** Facts or data may be regarded as raw materials for the rational manager who is trying to do a scientific job of management. That is, the scientific manager attempts to search for the truth. To see where the "weight of evidence" will lead him, the scientific manager wants not only facts but also an abundance of relevant facts which are as free from bias as possible. However, the scientific manager must be cautious. First, he may become so engrossed in the accumulation of masses of data that he forgets to ask himself what he will do with the collected data. Fortunately, the practical limitations of organizational factors such as time, cost, or other resources should help to prevent the mature manager from going off the deep end too often while engaged in the sometimes desperate task of collecting data. Also, in his search for truth the manager must discriminate between relevant and irrelevant facts, and between assumption and opinion. In this connection, it should be noted that although facts are universal, interpretations of facts are personal. The rational manager should be aware that his analysis of facts tends to be dominated to an extent by his conceptual framework or system of ideas which is the product of his years of background, education, and experience. The concepts and ideas that he brings to the facts influence their relevance and significance. Thus, the scientific manager should be careful and make every attempt to be as logical and as objective as possible in dealing with the data at hand. He should especially avoid the attempt to establish some favorite idea by choosing only that data which will support his contention or "prove" his decision. Finally, a manager should try to avoid the manufacturing of facts. This takes place when he has already prejudged a situation and wishes to build a case for his "decision of desire" by providing an illusory factual base.

Because of the limitations of the human mind in comprehending and interpreting large masses of data, the deliberate manager must boil down his data to a manageable state. This involves a number of steps. In addition to the observation of data in the collection process, facts must be described. "Observed facts" are undescribed facts; they are perceived but are not yet put into symbols. The moment they are conceptualized and expressed in words, "observed facts" become "described facts." This is an abstraction process in which the observed sensory impressions are translated into verbal, numerical, or other symbolic form. Facts are described so that they may be communicated and thus made capable of analysis by the researcher and others. In addition to the important tasks of collecting and describing data, the rational manager must also classify or categorize the data, record his data in written or printed form, and summarize his data by statistical or judgmental means—the necessary stages in the refinement of facts. It should be kept in mind that this chain of steps in the refining process is very important to the quality of the managerial decisions or actions which are based upon the facts. Accordingly, the quality of the refined data will depend upon the quality of the observed raw data; the refined data will be no better than the poorest item in the chain of steps in the refining process; and, finally, the managerial decisions or actions can be no better than the quality of the refined data or facts upon which they are based.

INFERENCES

The interpretation of empirical experience is, however, only the beginning of the scientific method. The rational manager must use inference or generalization—in addition to the observation and collection of facts, the abstraction process in which facts are described, the classification of facts, and the recording and summarization of facts. Through his analysis of the facts and the relationships discovered among facts or classes of facts, the manager gains insight into the material truth of his data and is now in a position to make generalizations from the facts. Such generalizations are in the nature of inferences or inductions which he has abstracted from his mass of facts and which he supposes may be universally or generally true. This ascent by inference from data or facts to one or more generalizations is a psychological process, in which the individual intellectually moves from facts to generalizations. It takes a thinking manager to infer something from the facts. He cannot be sure that the generalizations are valid until he has put the tentatively formulated inferences to some adequate test. This testing requirement brings the use of *models* into the scientific method. Models are very important in scientific work, in scientific management, and in almost any intellectual endeavor. An understanding of the nature and role of the model is thus essential to an adequate understanding of the scientific method.

MODELS

A model may be defined, for our purposes, as an approximation or representation of reality. It is not reality itself—if it were, then the model and reality would be identical and, consequently, there would be no need for a model. Examples of physical models range from girls' dolls or boys' model airplanes to wind tunnels used by scientists. It should be noted that the model is exemplified in this sense as a replica (model airplane) of an original (full-sized aircraft). It is not necessary, and frequently not possible, that the model reproduce every characteristic of the original. Through the process of abstraction, only a few of the characteristics may be duplicated in the model so that attention and study may be focused on a somewhat more simple phenomenon. If one wishes to analyze further, these omitted details may be studied in another or more complex model.

In addition to physical models, there are various other types of models. Some models assert logical relationships and may be called logical models. Generalizations or inferences from facts frequently serve as premises in a variety of such logical models. Other models are mathematical (symbolic) in nature wherein mathematical relationships are established among variables. Models may also be descriptive or abstract, in which case they are developed as verbal models to replace physical models, to describe facts, or to represent concepts, ideas, generalizations, or inferences. Moreover, the notion of probability may be introduced in statistical models. Finally, there are chemical, biological, psychological, economic, sociological, and many other types of models. Models may also use combinations of ideas of various fields of knowledge so that the manager may utilize all possible facets in attempting to obtain practical results from his analysis.

The relationship between the world of models and the real world is illustrated by the following diagram (Figure 4-1).

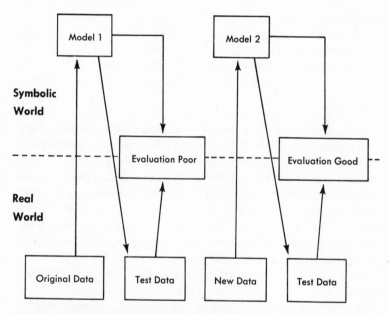

FIGURE 4-1. **Models and reality.** Developed from Irwin D. Bross, *Design for Decision* (New York: Macmillan, 1953), Figures 10.01 and 10.02, pp. 174, 177.

While a model can be anything the manager desires it to be for practical purposes, it is generally stimulated by data or facts from the real world. A variety of models becomes possible when the manager's concepts and imagination are added. If a manager is adept at description or logic, then descriptive and logical models become possible. If the manager has any quantitative sophistication, or if he has someone on his staff who has, then mathematical and/or statistical models are possible, and so on.

Once a model has been created there are two lines of development—one in the symbolic world and one in the real world.

In the symbolic world the model's implications are pursued by manipulation of the language or symbols used in the model. Thus, the nature and complexity of the model seriously affects its development. After some development of the model in the symbolic world, the insertion of test data (which may be a different type of data than the original) into the model is made to produce some result (s). If the results or application of the model to the real world do not turn out well (Figure 4-1), the whole process is repeated. Additional new data are acquired and another model developed and tested (Figure 4-1). This process is continued until truth is attained or until the manager has exhausted his available resources such as time and cost.

LIMITATIONS

Perhaps by now the reader has already observed that a wide gulf separates the rule-of-thumb and autocratic methods of management from the scientific method. The rule-of-thumb method involves the uncritical acceptance of conclusions, tends to be unsympathetic toward facts, and is fearful of testing. The autocratic method is a pretentious one in which the autocrat is inclined to be impatient and is more concerned with subjectivity than objectivity. It seems, therefore, that the scientific method is preferable. It is rational; the other two methods are not. Yet, even this method is not without drawbacks. What are its limitations?

In the first place, the use of the scientific method requires a critical mind which all managers do not possess. It can be used only by those individuals who are objective, fact demanding, orderly, logical, discerning, honest, and free from tradition. To develop such a critical mind, managers must acquire knowledge and experience and make an effort to avoid intellectual rigidity or dogmatism. In the second place, the scientific method can be time consuming. A manager's decisions and actions cannot always wait for the scientific method to run its course. Sometimes problematic situations in organizations demand quick or even instantaneous decisions so that it may be better to risk being wrong than to be indecisive or inactive. Luckily the scientific method is quite useful in the majority of organizational decisions or actions, because the demand for quick de-.

cisions is not generally characteristic of organizations. Moreover, this second limitation can be overcome to a large extent through repetitious practice by managers in the use of the scientific method. It is impressive to note how quickly one can develop facility and speed in the use of the scientific method. Such efforts by managers are of great value, since managers develop an unusual ability to solve problems rationally and to react intelligently and quickly in emergencies.

Management by Participation

Management by participation, sometimes called consultative management, leadership management, democratic management, or participative management, grows out of the conviction that individuals respond best in organizations when they can *participate* in the process of management, especially decision-making, in matters that affect them. While this philosophy is still fairly rare in the United States, it is propounded by a growing number of authorities on management.[2] Douglas McGregor found that unrealistic asumptions about people by management were the cause of many failures of expensive plans. These are the assumptions of his Theory X, the traditional view of direction and control, and may be summarized as follows: most people are lazy and dislike work, lack self-control, must be coerced, and are unable to think for themselves. It is easy to see why many operating plans of management failed as cooperation quickly disappeared when management began to coerce and threaten to get its decisions executed.

On the other hand, McGregor's Theory Y proposes to use authoritarian methods of control only when absolutely necessary. The assumptions of Theory Y, the integration of individual and organizational goals, may be summarized as follows: people are capable of developing a mature and responsible attitude toward work, they are not inherently lazy, work is as natural as rest and recreation, they should be given opportunity to make decisions and to follow their own style of working, they should be given an opportunity to discuss and understand the reasons for conformity, positive motivation is superior to negative moti-

[2] See, for example, Douglas McGregor, *The Human Side of Enterprise* (New York: McGraw-Hill, 1960), especially Chapters 3 and 4 and pp. 244-246.

vation (threat or punishment), and ego satisfaction and self-realization are as important or more important to the individual than the dollar. In other words, Theory Y is a way of getting people to do what they should be doing because they want to do it rather than because someone else has made it clear that they must do it. Here management takes the initiative in securing genuine participation through prior consultation with people at different organizational levels to get reactions to proposed decisions or courses of action. This may require greater delegation of authority and responsibility as well as the careful selection and use of committees to encourage cooperation and participative decision-making at all levels. Such an approach would require that many organizations undergo a complete reorientation of their managerial philosophy in dealing with workers. Managers would have to become *leaders* with competence in interpersonal relations rather than autocrats, rule-of-thumbers, functionaries, or rule makers. Finally, when management by participation is combined with management by the scientific method, the best possible combination of methods emerges. Individual managers would thus rationally approach their decisions according to the scientific method but would permit participation to be a qualifying factor, since the decisions and actions of even rational managers must be accepted and carried out by other human beings. Thus, the recognition of subordinates as executors and implementors of management's decisions and actions clearly points up the value of participation as a method of management.

THE FUNCTIONS OF ORGANIZATIONS

Earlier, management was defined as that activity in an organization which consists of deciding upon the goals of an organization and of deciding upon the means by which the goals are to be reached. Once the goals of an organization have been decided upon, managers are concerned with the function of the means—personnel and capital—in the *operating* activities of purchasing, producing, marketing, financing, accounting, research and development, and facilitating. The managing of the personnel and capital engaged in these operating functions is the reason for the existence of management. Consequently, a brief inquiry into the nature and scope of both the operating and managing functions should give the reader a good idea of what is involved in the management of organizations.

The Operating Functions[3]

PURCHASING

Purchasing or buying is the procurement of goods or services of any kind or of rights through the exchange of property. Included in this broad concept of purchasing would be the buying of raw materials or parts for production or manufacture; the procurement of finished merchandise for resale; the purchase of supplies, furniture, fixtures, equipment, land and buildings; and the acquisition of rights such as patents, copyrights, franchises, and even goodwill. In order to make a bona fide purchase, one point must be kept clearly in mind—there must be an exchange of property for the item (s) purchased. If property is not given up, there is no purchase. Thus, if a city or town gives a piece of land to a company to encourage it to locate a new plant there, it is not a purchase but a gift, because no property is given up in exchange for the land. With respect to actual purchases, the purchasing agent or procurement officer should make every effort in his negotiations to adhere to the criterion of cost and quality to secure goods which are best suited to the objectives at hand at the lowest cost, rather than to purchase those of the highest quality. Waste, obsolescence, and speculation should also be avoided, whereas "hedging"—taking a position on both the cash and the futures sides of the market—is permitted in order to protect an organization from losses due to price fluctuations during the processing period between the purchase of raw materials (for example, sugar) and the sale of the finished product (for example, jams and jellies). Finally, excluded from the concept of purchasing are management activities such as the preparation of purchasing budgets and the comparison of actual

[3] Since extended treatment of the operating functions does not come within the scope of this book, the reader should consult specialized texts such as those at the end of this chapter in each area if he wishes additional information.

expenditures with budget appropriations to determine variations and what to do about them.

PRODUCING

Producing may be defined as that operating function which creates goods and services. Producing yields utility or the capacity to satisfy customers' wants and includes a great variety of activities, depending upon the nature of the organization. For example, in a factory or plant, producing activities would include such manufacturing processes as casting, hot and cold treatment and forming of metals, machining, painting, and assembling. In a retail store, the producing function would include whatever is done to accommodate customers such as ventilation, elevators, counters, wrapping, rest rooms, and so forth. In a hospital, producing activities include whatever is undertaken to aid patients by way of surgery, nursing, transfusing, sterilizing, preparing of special foods, and the like.

MARKETING

Marketing includes all activities involved in the movement of goods and services from production to consumption. As such, marketing is not limited to the physical distribution of goods and services, but also includes attempts to increase total demand in the economy by sales promotion and advertising. Thus, marketing as broadly conceived would include making potential customers aware of a need, demonstrating how this need may be satisfied, and providing the means of satisfaction through such activities as storage, grading, transportation, packing, servicing, and so forth. Moreover, marketing embraces all types of selling such as field selling, direct mail selling, counter selling, house selling, and floor selling. Finally, excluded from the marketing function are activities suggested by marketing management or sales management.

FINANCING

Financing is that function which consists of obtaining and utilizing the assets or property necessary for the efficient operation of an organization. Basically, this amounts to seeing that cash is on hand to pay bills as they become due, and to assisting in the maximization of the long-run financial goal of profit or return on investment. In order to have cash on hand to pay maturing bills, the treasurer must have available a variety of sources of funds such as profits, loans, credit, and securities. Financial institutions and security exchanges thus take on considerable importance. Also, once the funds are acquired, the treasurer is faced with the fine art of effectively using the funds by way of capital flow, internal control, working capital turnover, financial analysis, and investment analysis. As custodian of the organization's assets, he must see that all funds and all other types of assets are intact. He alone is responsible for the negotiation, acquisition, and effective utilization of funds and assets. Liquidity or lack of liquidity as a part of the asset structure of an organization is his problem and requires the closest surveillance.

ACCOUNTING

Accounting as the recording, classifying, summarizing, and interpreting of transactions in monetary terms is one of the most important functions of any organization. Written chronological records (journals) tell us *when* transactions took place while summarizing records (ledgers) tell us *how much* of any asset, liability, or net worth item the organization possesses. Such information is invaluable to management, investors, bankers, other creditors, and government agencies. Moreover, such summarizing of financial data is necessary to determine net income and taxable income. Once financial transactions are summarized in a trial balance or list of account balances, the accountant is ready to make whatever adjustments are necessary to permit the preparation of financial statements such as the profit-and-loss-statement, the balance sheet, equity statements, the cost-of-goods-manufactured statement, the application-of-funds statement, and so on. In addition to the more traditional activities of accounting leading up to financial statements and their interpretation, the modern accountant is expected not only to provide management with up-to-date historical data, but also to provide management with estimated future cost data useful to management in the decision-making process. Because cost considerations enter into almost all organizational decisions, and since decisions always concern the future and not the past, the accounting function can render a real service to management.

RESEARCH AND DEVELOPMENT

The operating function of research and development includes those activities which lead to the attainment of knowledge, and the translation of that knowledge into a useful product, service, process, or technique. The stages of research and development are (1) basic research, (2) the origin of the practical idea, (3) applied research, (4) development, and (5) testing and evaluation.[4] Basic research provides the foundation for the insight or enlightenment necessary for the discovery of the practical idea. Applied research then determines the best methods by which the practical idea is to be developed. Development involves experimental work to put the concept into operational form. Finally, testing and evaluation involves modifications and improvements in form to enhance performance or utility so that the new product, service, process, device, or technique can be sold and/or used. Through these stages, the goals of research and development are achieved—an essential aspect of survival and growth in a dynamic economy.

FACILITATING

The operating function known as *facilitating* may be envisioned as a catch-all function. As such, it **includes all and any activities found in organizations which exist to serve, aid, or support the other operating functions and the functions of management.** Thus, those activities which do not fit into the operating functions of purchasing, producing, marketing, financing, accounting, research and development, or into the managing functions, are considered as facilitating. Facilitating functions include all kinds of maintenance, day- and night-watching, legal activities, janitorial work, policing, data processing, stenographic and clerical activities, heating, and the like. While these activities may fall into our catch-all category of facilitating, it should not be assumed that they are not significant. On the contrary, the facilitating functions are very important to an organization—in

---

[4] Waino Suojanen, *The Dynamics of Management* (New York: Holt, 1966) pp. 29-30.

some cases of critical importance. Consider, for example, the effects of poor maintenance on machinery in a plant, or the results of poor or inadequate heating in a hospital, or the results of the sudden malfunction of computers. Indeed, the impact of the latter could cause industrial systems to grind to a halt; banks, hospitals, educational institutions, business firms, and other organizations like the Internal Revenue Service would begin to bulge with unprocessed paper; air travel would be chaotically disrupted. Such possible outcomes should quickly impress upon the reader that while facilitating has been considered as the last operating function for the purpose of analysis, we cannot assume it to be the least.

The Functions of Management

DECISION-MAKING: THE ESSENCE OF MANAGEMENT

In the field of management there has been a considerable amount of discussion among the traditionalists as to the proper sequence of the management functions. Some take the position that the planning function must come before organizing, directing, and controlling because planning determines in advance what should be done. I wish to agree with this, but at the same time wish to put forth the proposition that decision-making must precede planning because plans are made up of decisions. To put it another way, plans are the result of decisions. As a matter of fact, many decisions are necessary before a plan is made. One decision calls for another until there is a train of decisions leading to the plan. Moreover, decisions leading to one plan must not conflict with those leading to another, for conflicting decisions and plans will lead to either poor or no coordination. Obviously the decision-making function of management is basic. But, as we shall see presently, even organizing, directing, and controlling depend upon intelligent decision-making because no one can do anything in any of these areas without making decisions. Organizing, directing, and controlling require making many decisions to establish an effective organization, motivated direction, and a high level of control. Thus, the decision-making function is fundamental in all management and this is why we shall treat it first.

Decision-making is an affirmative or negative intellectual assertion or judgment among alternative ends or among alternative means to achieve some end. In this sense, decision-making is not to be confused with other methods such as habit, impulse, emotion, rule-of-thumb, or chance, which are not intellectual. While I am aware that others call these "decision-making" methods, they have been deliberately excluded by definition for the purpose of our analysis.

Decision-making deals with problems and alternatives. Whether the decision-maker chooses one alternate or another depends upon many factors. First, there is his ability to reason validly. Mastery of logical analysis enables a decision-maker to get a firm hold on a difficult management problem. Second, the philosophical aspects of deciding cannot be overlooked in a society which is becoming more and more sensitive to ethics and morality in industry and organizations. Third, a prudent decision-maker must be aware of the behavioral side of decision-making. Decisions are not made in a vacuum. Modern psychology has contributed materially to our knowledge of the conditions and factors which influence the thought processes in action. The influence of culture as a conditioning factor in decision-making is not to be ignored. Moreover, when a manager makes a decision that affects the behavior of others, he sets social processes in motion. A manager cannot overlook the fact that his decisions are made in a social framework. Fourth, the importance of quantitative elements in decision-making has increased greatly since World War II. Here, the decision-maker needs to be aware of such areas as fact finding and processing, models and model building, prediction and probability, and mathematical and statistical analysis. Finally, organizational and strategic elements in decision-making cannot be slighted by the rational decision-maker.

THE TRADITIONAL FUNCTIONS OF MANAGEMENT

Much of what was said about decision-making in the preceding section would have been called planning by many of the classical writers in management. The view in this text is that planning is an *area* of decision-making—in other words, what managers actually do in planning is to make planning decisions. Some of the basic planning decisions that managers may make include (1) policy decisions regarding personnel, product or service quality policy decisions, manufacturing policy decisions, maintenance policy decisions, accounting policy decisions, collection policy decisions, price, advertising and merchandise policy decisions, and engineering design policy decisions; (2) master planning decisions such as budgetary decisions; (3) detailed planning decisions such as procedures and standards; and (4) strategic decisions in planning involving the mobilization of followers and the exploitation of opportunity. As much as possible in an organization should be planned in advance of what should be done, especially when we realize that it is the *unplanned* things in organizational life, as well as in personal life, that trip us up and frequently result in serious errors and loss of property and/or other values.

Decisions and plans, however well thought out and written down, cannot execute themselves. An *organization* is necessary if plans are to be carried out. Since an organization is the result of organizing decisions, we can immediately see the importance of such decisions to any enterprise. Organizing involves the grouping of activities into well defined jobs and departments; the acquisition of personnel and capital appropriate for jobs; the establishment of line, staff, functional, and other relationships among jobs; the assignment of personnel and capital to jobs; the training of personnel; and the delegation of authority and responsibility. With the delegation of authority, the organization is now ready to act as a tool in the execution of decisions and plans. However, an organization places some limits upon the manager. It would indeed be impractical to make decisions and develop plans which are beyond the capacity of the organization to execute. Moreover, once an organization is established it cannot always be quickly altered to accomodate every change in decisions and plans. Accordingly, the manager must bear in mind that, for the execution of decisions and plans, the organization is a limiting factor.

Once decisions and plans have been made and an organization established, the next step is to cause or stimulate the organization to act according to plan. This involves directing decisions— motivation decisions, communication decisions, and other leader-

ship decisions. It is the manager's job to use motivating means
such as monetary and nonmonetary incentives to influence and
persuade personnel to do willingly what is expected of them as
members of an organization. As leaders of men, managers should
learn to communicate with precision to subordinates, as well as
to associates and superiors. In addition, managers should make
every effort to understand followers, never to forget their roles
as leaders, and to develop the ability to deal effectively with opposition and resistance as difficulties arise in their relationships
with subordinates, associates, and superiors. If the above activities
are well performed, the outcome will be the desirable condition
of **motivated direction—the desire of the members of an organization to do what is expected of them.**

Once the wheels of an organization start turning, it is necessary to see that activities and events proceed as previously
decided and planned. This involves the making of *controlling decisions* which include measurement decisions, comparison decisions, and correction decisions. Here again the importance of
planning decisions should be emphasized. It would be impossible
to check on whether or not an organization is functioning according to plans if there were no plans, norms, or standards
against which to measure. When actual behavior in an organization does not agree with planned behavior, it is only through
quantitative and/or qualitative measurement and comparison
that departures, deviations, or variances can be detected and
corrected. Although the terms "controlling" and "control" are
frequently used synonymously, I view **control as the outcome of
controlling decisions,** and refer to a condition in which the decisions and actions of nonmanagers or operatives approximate
in some degree the decisions and actions that managers would
make in the same situation. When a high level of control exists
in an organization, deviations from planning decisions, as discovered through measurement decisions and comparison decisions, will be much less significant. Consequently, the corrective
and remedial action necessary to raise the level of control will
be minimized. Finally, when all of the management functions
are adequately and effectively performed, the result will be
coordination, a most desirable and sought after general condition of good management.

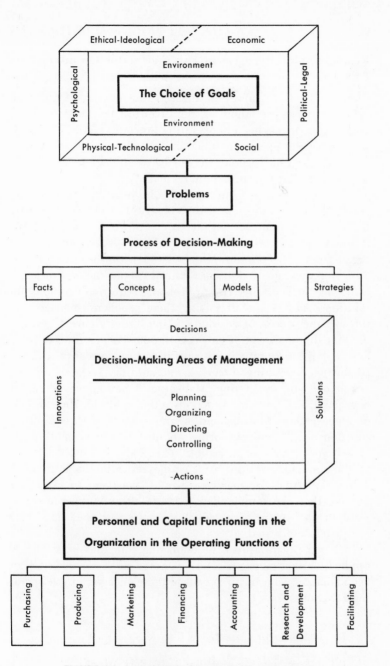

FIGURE 4-2. **A conceptual framework for management.**

Relationship of Management Functions to the Operating Functions

After this brief survey of the separate operating and managing functions, we might ask ourselves this pertinent question: How are the managing and operating functions related? To begin with, since the operating functions and the management functions are parts of a whole, we can be assured that they are not only related but are intimately related.

The integration of a number of concepts developed in chapters 2, 3, and 4 of this text can be observed in Figure 4-2. At the top of the diagram we see the choice of goals made within a complex environment. But once goals are decided upon in an organization, the organization is faced with the difficulties of achieving these goals. The uncertainties about the best means of achieving the goals give rise to problems requiring decisions and solutions. As a means of solving these problems, managers act through the process of decision-making. From Figure 4-2 we can see that the managers of an organization manage the personnel and capital functioning in the operating functions of purchasing, producing, marketing, financing, accounting, research and development, and facilitating. Managing of personnel and capital engaged in the operating functions is the reason for the existence of management. Management becomes effective through these functions, and thus can bring about the achievement of the chosen goals of the organization. The goals are finally achieved by the nonmanagers (operative employees) who make the kinds of decisions that the managers would like them to make, not because they are commanded to make them but because they want to do what is expected of them because they have been adequately motivated.

In larger organizations the managing functions must also be applied to other managers. Here, as noted earlier, managers manage managers, who in turn manage those engaged in the operating functions.

Discussion Questions

1. What is management? What is its derivation?

2. What are the traditional functions of management? Why is the specific number of functions not a matter of great significance?

3. Distinguish between management and administration as held by some people in industry. Is this a legitimate distinction? What is the position taken in the text?

4. Is management a science? Discuss. Is management an art? Discuss.

5. What is the purpose of management?

6. What are the possible meanings of the term "theory"? What is a principle of management? Does a college or university train "finished executives"?

7. List the methods of management. What are the features of the rule-of-thumb method of management?

8. What is meant by "management by autocracy"?

9. What are the essential characteristics of management by the scientific method?

10. What is the role of facts in the scientific method of management? What is meant by manufacturing the facts?

11. What is an inference? What is a model?

12. How are models used in the method of science? Why are they used?

13. What are the limitations of management by the scientific method?

14. Compare rule-of-thumb management and autocratic management with management by the scientific method.

15. What is the meaning of "management by participation"? By what other names is this method of management called?

16. What are the functions of organizations? What are the operating functions of organizations?

17. Define the following terms: purchasing, producing, marketing, research and development, financing, accounting, and facilitating.

18. Define decision-making. What is the view taken in this text with respect to the traditional functions of management?

19. What is the relationship of the managing functions to the operating functions?

20. What class of functions will not receive extended treatment in this book? Why?

References

Begeman, Myron L., *Manufacturing Processes,* 3rd ed. (New York: Wiley, 1952), Chapters 2-19.

Bross, Irwin D. J., *Design for Decision* (New York: Macmillan, 1953), Chapters 1-6, 8-14.

Dale, Ernest, *Management: Theory and Practice* (New York: McGraw-Hill, 1965), Part 1.

Davis, Ralph C., *The Fundamentals of Top Management* (New York: Harper, 1951), Chapters 3, 8-14, 17-19.

Duddy, Edward A., and David A. Revzan, *Marketing* (New York: McGraw-Hill, 1947), Parts I-V.

Finney, H. A., and H. E. Miller, *Principles of Accounting,* 4th ed. (Englewood Cliffs: Prentice-Hall, 1953), Volumes I-III.

Flippo, Edwin B., *Principles of Personnel Management* (New York: McGraw-Hill, 1961), Chapters 3-6.

Haimann, Theo, *Professional Management* (Boston: Houghton Mifflin, 1962), Chapter 2.

Hardwick, C. T., and B. F. Landuyt, *Administrative Strategy* (New York: Simmons-Boardman, 1961), Chapters 1, 2.

Johnson, Robert W., *Financial Management* (Boston: Allyn & Bacon, 1959), Parts I-IV.

Lewis, Howard T., *Procurement* (Homewood: Irwin, 1948), Chapters 3-14, 17.

McGregor, Douglas, *The Human Side of Enterprise* (New York: McGraw-Hill, 1960), Chapters 3-6, 8-12.

Maier, N. R. F., *Principles of Human Relations* (New York: Wiley, 1955), Chapters 1, 3.

Mooney, James D., *The Principles of Organization,* rev. ed. (New York: Harper, 1947), Chapter 1.

Newman, William H., and C. E. Summer, Jr., *The Process of Management,* 2nd. ed. (Englewood Cliffs: Prentice-Hall, 1967), Chapters 1, 2.

Terry, George R., *Principles of Management,* 3rd ed. (Homewood: Irwin, 1960), Chapters 1, 2, 5.

Chapter 5. **The Problem of Choice**

Definitions
>   Decision, Judgment, and Choice
>   Deciding and Decision-Making

Occasions for Choice
>   Cases Originating with Superiors, Associates, and Subordinates
>   Cases Detected through Observation and Perception
>   Cases Detected through Investigation and Research

Aspectional Approaches to Choice
>   Philosophical Aspects
>>   Ethics
>>   Prudence
>>   Justice
>   Behavorial Aspects
>>   Economics
>>   Psychology
>>   Sociology
>>   Anthropology
>   Logical Aspects
>>   Premises and Implications
>>   Induction and Deduction
>   Quantitative Aspects
>>   Abstraction
>>   Model Building
>>   Quantitative Representation

Discussion Questions

References

Chapter 5

The Problem of Choice

Decision is a sharp knife that cuts clean and straight;
indecision, a dull one that hacks and tears
and leaves ragged edges behind it.—Gordon Graham

As already mentioned, planning leans heavily upon decision-making because plans are made up of decisions. Similarly, organizing, directing, and controlling depend significantly upon the activity of decision-making because in the performance of these functions it is necessary to make many important and vital decisions. Hence, the statement that decision-making is a fundamental and universal activity of the manager now begins to take on meaning.

However management writers and practitioners define a manager's function, there is general agreement that one of the chief functions of a manager, executive, administrator, or supervisor at any hierarchical level in an organization is to make decisions. This has been true as long as we have had organizations, it is true today, and it will undoubtedly be true in the future because man, unlike other animals who live by instinct, is a deciding animal. While decision-making may be responsible for many of man's worries, anxieties, tensions, pressures, gray hairs, ulcers, and neuroses, it is also responsible for his domination of this planet and perhaps even of other parts of the universe in the future.

In spite of its extraordinary significance, the subject of choice has received little attention until recently. Only during the past three decades has the topic been seriously discussed in the literature and at management conferences and conventions. If decision-making lies at the heart of administration, it would seem that a great deal can be learned by analyzing the process and making both managers and nonmanagers conscious of it. Some executives have been remarkably candid about their own ability to analyze decision-making—usually they admit that they just don't know how they do it. Charles Cox, president of Kennecott Copper, says: "I don't think businessmen know how they make decisions. I know I don't." Benjamin Fairless, former chairman of United States Steel, says: "You don't know how you do it; you just do it." Dwight Joyce, president of Glidden Company, states: "If a vice-president asks me how I was able to choose the right course, I have to say, I'm damned if I know."[1] This uncertainty about the decision-making process unfortunately detracts from the confidence placed in the decisions of managers —the leaders of organizations. We can only speculate about the higher standard of living that could accrue to us if managers made better decisions which would result in greater efficiency, lower costs, increased quality, and reduced prices.

In the past we have seen important advances in organization theory and practice, in personnel management and human relations, in management training, in economic analysis, in financial and accounting methodology, in marketing research and more recently in decision-making. This has resulted in significant improvements in our managerial competence. In the future the emphasis in management will be on the further understanding of decision-making in its logical, behavioral, qualitative and quantitative aspects. The manager who presently gets by with little or no knowledge of the process of decision-making will have to understand and use it in the future, with the result of an even greater improvement in managerial performance.

DEFINITIONS

Decision, Judgment, and Choice

Since decision-making is such an important and pervasive activity of a manager, what is a decision? The dictionary meaning of the word "decision" is that it is a conclusion or termination of a process. It is "the act of deciding; determination, as of a question or controversy; a judgment, as one formally pronounced by

[1] John McDonald, "How Businessmen Make Decisions," *Fortune*, LII, No. 2 (August, 1955), p. 85.

a court; a making up of one's mind; a resolution; also, the quality of being decided; firmness, as of character."[2] The term is also defined by many professionals such as management writers, economists, and psychologists.

Many writers have taken great pains to distinguish "decision" from "habit." George Katona, exemplifying the point of view of a psychologist-economist, presents the following formulation:

Genuine decisions . . . require the perception of a new situation and the solution of the problem raised by it: they lead to responding to a situation in a new way. In contrast, habitual behavior is rather common. We do what we did before in a similar situation . . . The main point is that the psychological process involved is different from that in genuine decision. Routine behavior, or using rules of thumb, are suitable terms to describe the second form of behavior.[3]

Chester I. Barnard, former president of the New Jersey Bell Telephone Company, sums up the findings of many writers most succinctly:

The acts of individuals may be distinguished in principle as those which are the result of deliberation, calculation, thought, and those which are unconscious, automatic, responsive, the results of internal or external conditions present or past. In general, whatever processes precede the first class of acts culminate in what may be termed 'decision.'[4]

Barnard appears to be classifying human behavior. His statement may be interpreted as suggesting that human behavior results from either conscious or unconscious processes; and when these processes are conscious, they culminate in decision. The second, unconscious or automatic class, may well be called "habit." Most writers emphasize this distinction between conscious and unconscious action, the voluntary and the involuntary, although a few such as Herbert A. Simon[5] maintain that if the individual follows one course of action there are other courses

---

[2] *The New Century Dictionary.*

[3] George Katona, *Psychological Aanalysis of Economic Behavior,* 1st ed. (New York: McGraw-Hill, 1951) , p. 49.

[4] Chester I. Barnard, *The Functions of the Executive* (Cambridge: Harvard University Press, 1938) , p. 185.

[5] Herbert A. Simon, *Administrative Behavior* (New York: Macmillan, 1947) , p. 4.

of action that he foregoes, and thereby makes a "decision" even though it be merely a reflex action such as striking a particular key on a typewriter. In this latter sense, the term "decision" is used without any implication of a necessary conscious or deliberate process.

Many other management writers have also tried to define "decision."[6] In their presentations, as in others', there appears to exist, either expressed or implied, a keynote idea—the selection of one alternative from among two or more alternatives. This keynote idea leads to a number of inferences: (1) a selection of one alternative from among two or more alternatives is either a selection among goals (ends) or a selection among means; (2) a choice among alternatives implies a process of appraisal in which reasons for and against the alternatives are considered, and which eventually culminates in a judgment—an assertive (affirmative or negative) intellectual act. Based upon these two statements, a *decision* may then be thought of for our purposes as **an affirmative or negative intellectual assertion or judgment among alternative ends or among alternative means to achieve some end.** Also, although the terms "decision" and "decision-making" are sometimes used as synonyms, it seems best to me that the term "decision" be reserved as the outcome or end result of "decision-making"—**the thought process that precedes but terminates in decision.** Thus, the outcome of decision-making is decision. Finally, the terms "choice" and "judgment" will be used synonymously with the term "decision" in the following discussion.

Deciding and Decision-Making

Since we have agreed that "decision-making" refers to a manager's thought processes that precede decision, where does the term "deciding" fit into our scheme of ideas? The answer is that "deciding" is a synonym for decision-making and the two terms may be used interchangeably. Both terms refer to the process

---

[6] See, for example, George R. Terry, 3rd ed., *Principles of Management* (Homewood: Irwin, 1960), p. 43; Richard N. Owens, *Introduction to Business Policy* (Homewood: Irwin, 1954), p. 115; Charles Jamison, *Business Policy* (Englewood Cliffs: Prentice-Hall, 1953), p. 120; Manley H. Jones, *Executive Decision-Making* (Homewood: Irwin, 1957), p. 5.

that precedes and culminates in decision or judgment. Similarly, the terms "decision-maker" and "decider," referring to the one engaged in decision-making or deciding, shall be used synonymously.

OCCASIONS FOR CHOICE

To suppose that decision-making is mainly the function of top-level managers is a gross misconception. All managers make decisions. What is more, all nonmanagers or operatives also make decisions. The role of the manager as one who decides and manages subordinates so that they will make the kind of decisions he would like them to make is a most important one. The achievement of the goals of any organization depends upon it. But a manager cannot engage in the process of deciding unless he is aware of situations or problems which call for decisions. This is why we must now examine the occasions for choice.

Cases Originating with Superiors, Associates, and Subordinates

From the study of psychology we know that a human being cannot respond to stimuli unless he is aware of such stimuli. Thus, managers cannot be aware of problems or situations demanding decisions without focusing upon some internal or external stimulus which produces a conscious idea or thought. It is extremely important, therefore, that managers be attentive to all problematic situations so that they are aware of the need to engage in the activity of decision-making.

How do managers become aware of cases in which a decision is needed? There are a number of ways. First, a manager may be forced into making a decision because authority and responsibility have been delegated to him by his superior (s) . A written report, an oral communication, an order, an instruction, or the failure of an adopted plan may be all that is necessary to make a manager aware of a case for choice. Second, an associate at luncheon may bring his attention to certain events, mistakes, uncertainties, conflicting orders or instructions, or other interferences that may call for immediate judgment. Third, a subordinate may telephone him to say that he would like to discuss some puzzling matter which, because of its novelty or uniqueness, he feels relatively incompetent to handle. This is an example of the *exception principle,* which states that simple matters may be delegated to subordinates, whereas more difficult matters should be referred to those at a higher managerial level who are qualified to deal with the problem. Finally, it should be mentioned that managers' awareness of cases originating with superiors, associates, and subordinates is greatly facilitated if there is a free flow of communication in the organization, both vertically between superiors and subordinates and horizontally among associates.

Cases Detected through Observation and Perception

The manager may also become aware of problems needing decisions through his own direct observation and perception. The manager of a retail store may spend a great deal of time in the store just watching and observing; the production manager of a plant may walk through the factory to see how things are going; an office manager frequently may look up from his work at his employees; a sales manager may go into the field to see how his salesmen are doing; a hospital administrator may walk through corridors and visit departments; or an educational administrator may notice a man bowing his head in thought, a man's aloofness, an inconsistency in conversation, or a certain tenseness in the academic atmosphere. Finally, observation and perception also consists of examining reports, reviewing documents, and scrutinizing quantitative measures of the organization's performance.

Cases Detected through Investigation and Research

A really alert and dynamic manager should not be content with communications from others and his own observation and perception to uncover problematic situations. On the contrary, he should also go out and look for these situations. A manager must be a detective, a watch dog, searching for problems and uncertainties that need or will need resolution. Thus, he and/or his staff must engage in scientific inquiry and research which will give him the knowledge he needs to uncover problem areas, which are difficult or impossible to unearth by the more pedestrian methods of communication systems and observation.

Fundamentally, there are just two areas where problems requiring choice may be deliberately investigated and researched: (1) in the environment of organizations; and (2) within the operating and managerial parts of the organization itself. In the environment of an organization, problems may exist in any of its six phases: ethical-ideological, political-legal, economic, social, psychological, and physical-technological. These environmental influences were all covered in Chapter 3. Within the organization itself, problematic situations may lurk in any of the seven operating areas or in any of the managerial decision areas. The seven operating areas of purchasing, producing, marketing, financing, accounting, research and development, and facilitating were examined from different points of view in both Chapters 2 and 4. The managerial decision areas of planning, organizing, directing, and controlling plus the seven operating areas are the principal directions of investigation and research and none of them should be overlooked.

ASPECTIONAL APPROACHES TO CHOICE

From the beginning of the twentieth century when Frederick W. Taylor ushered in "scientific management," there has been a steady evolution of thought in the field of management. This "mental revolution" is becoming more and more significant in American industry. Tradition in management is being displaced by rationality in management in new areas and in new ways. Consequently, an intellectual breakthrough is shedding some light on the process of decision-making—the cardinal function of management. Experts in human behavior are attempting to interpret the process in terms of their own specialties—philosophy, economics, psychology, sociology, anthropology, logic, statistics and mathematics. Accordingly, any inquiry into the function of decision-making requires that the relevant contributions of these specialists be considered.

Philosophical Aspects

The purpose of decision-making is the conscious selection among goals or the conscious direction of thought through the selection of means. In this connection, philosophers have concerned themselves mainly with the question of what constitutes a "good' decision—the major concern of moral philosophy. Because the objective of philosophy is the investigation of first causes[7] and since the decision-maker should be guided by right goals, the philosopher is vitally concerned with what the ends or goals of decision-making should be. Moreover, since a decision may also be a judgment among means to achieve some end, the philosopher is greatly concerned with the morality of the means chosen to achieve morally good ends. "Ethics," "prudence," and "justice" are the terms with which we are concerned and which will now be examined in some detail.

ETHICS

Man is a rational being. As such, in the Judaeo-Christian tradition, he contains a body and a soul. Man also possesses an intellect and a will. Because of this, man, unlike any other living creature on earth, is empowered with the freedom of judgment and choice. He alone in this world is able to choose, to decide, to judge. But this rare quality also carries responsibilities. A moral responsibility arises because man has a choice among alternatives. His ability to judge that some human actions are right and that some are wrong brings the moral problem of choice into clear focus. Some men consider these judgments of right and wrong so important that they will regulate their whole lives around them, and some will even sacrifice their lives rather than diverge from what they believe is right. On the other hand, society will punish and even put men to death when it thinks these men are not doing what they ought to do or are doing what they ought not to do. It is naive to say that morals or ethics are subjects for speculative philosophers and not for the practical organization man. For the man who does whatever he wants to do, with no regard for what he *ought* to do, is outlawed from society.

Ethics is concerned with the question of what is morally right or what is morally wrong. While the subject of ethics is speculative, it is also a practical study in its purpose and application.

[7] "First causes" are *ultimate* in the sense of being the last to be attained but the *first* to be known and desired. Charles C. Miltner, *The Elements of Ethics,* 2nd rev. ed. (New York: Macmillan, 1936), p. 21.

As a practical field of knowledge, ethics operates in the ever-changing real world. Since man's actions are forever new and changing, ethical standards are constantly changing with man and his culture. As a result, it is difficult to define this shifting moral responsibility. In any case, for our purposes, *ethics* may be defined as: **"The art or science of man's efforts to live in a proper harmonious relationship with other men, groups, or institutions; and the study of his moral responsibility to discern the rightness or wrongness of his actions."**[8] Thus, the individual has a basic responsibility for making ethical decisions.

In the interest of setting up standards for the governing of human behavior, society has developed a considerable complex of statute and common law. Since ethical decisions take place only in individuals' minds, legal regulations unfortunately do not entirely solve the moral problems of the community. Moreover, it is impractical to attempt to govern the ethical behavior of people or institutions by legislation. Nevertheless, the manager of an organization should constantly bear in mind that the ethical-ideological environment in the long run significantly influences the political-legal environment. Accordingly, what would normally be ethical today may be law tomorrow.

In textbooks, in novels, in television, in movies, and before Congressional committees, business has been attacked as evil and immoral. One would think that the problem of moral decay is the sole responsibility of business organizations. Actually, there are other segments of society that should be similarly judged. Sometimes the behavior of labor unions, government institutions, sports organizations, and entertainment operations could hardly be considered angelic. What is more, society has never precisely indicated what moral philosophy it would like business to follow. In other words, business does not have a *uniform code of ethics.* Even though a growing minority of managers is becoming sensitive to the moral issues facing their organizations, it should be remembered that business is composed of almost 5 million enterprises governed by men who have quite different backgrounds and values and who may be Christians, Jews, or atheists. As a result, these men have somewhat different concepts of what is

[8] J. Whitney Bunting, ed., *Ethics for Modern Business Practice* (Englewood Cliffs: Prentice-Hall, 1953), p. 5.

right. Consequently, the failure of business to maintain the proper ethical standards of conduct is partly the failure of society to provide the necessary ethical codes to be followed. Before attacking business for being immoral or amoral, society should first establish generally applicable ethical codes for proper organizational behavior. In any case, managers should make every effort possible to make *prudential* judgments based upon the principle of *justice*. This brings us to prudence and justice, the subjects of the next two sections.

PRUDENCE

The theory of ethics represents broad universal principles of moral right and wrong. While such moral principles may be sound, moral actions are individual, concrete events. When a man reasons about concrete and particular problems, he is being prudent. What, then, is prudence? **Prudence is that quality of the intellect which enables man to make moral decisions through reason.** Like any art, prudential skill requires practice. Man needs to develop and perfect his intellect by repeated acts and continued usage. As with the development of any complicated skill, progress is at first slow and painful but improves with repetition. With persistent practice, man can develop his intellect so that he can solve a concrete problem more quickly, more easily, and more accurately. In this regard, prudence deals with the means, not with the end (s) .

The process of making ethical decisions—reasoning from universal rules of good behavior—is complex and difficult. Fortunately, the prudent manager has a special skill which enables him to make ethical decisions promptly, accurately, and easily. But what is the nature of prudence? It is composed of three distinct operations: (1) to deliberate, think, or reason well; (2) to judge practically; (3) to execute, command, or implement reasonably. To deliberate well or to think well involves weighing the desirable and undesirable consequences of alternative means in relation to some end. To judge practically is to reach the decision that an alternative means is the best one. To execute, command, or implement is to see that decisions are carried out in reasonable ways. Secondly, in order to acquire foresight, circumspection, and caution—all essential elements of prudence—

practice and experience are necessary. Finally, on who possesses prudential skill recognizes that practical ethical decisions are variable and uncertain, and does his best to minimize uncertainty through reasoning, counsel, foresight, circumspection, and precaution.

JUSTICE

The term "justice" stems from the Latin word *justus,* which means right. **Justice refers to that which is right or just, or what is due to others.** Conversely, injustice does not respect the rights, dignity, rank, ability, worth, or merit of others. For example, a manager's rendering justice to his subordinates is his attempt to recognize ability and merit by means of a salary structure or fringe benefits based upon differences in qualifications and job productivity. Injustice is exemplified by an administrator who indiscriminately overlooks these differences. Such an administrator shows favoritism and partiality—acts of inequity.

If a man is to be just, he must be willing to give to others what is due them. This willingness may be called justice—a principle from which follow consistent acts that protect rights. It is not enough for a man to claim that the principle of justice is a valid one, and one that should be followed, if he does not practice justice himself. The world is full of people who say one thing and practice another. To be just is indeed difficult, for many times in professional or personal life men are almost viciously inclined to do what is unjust. To do the right or just thing frequently requires an act of the will, whereby a man's selfish inclinations are set aside.

There are several fundamental forms of justice which should interest managers. *Contractual or exchange justice* renders to the parties of a contract or agreement what is due them under the agreement. *Administrative or distributive justice* is an executive's disposition to render to each member of an organization (subordinates, associates, and superiors) that which is due him according to a proportionate equality. This means that the manager must consider both the value of the goods or money being distributed along with the unequal value or rank of the persons involved. *Legal justice* renders to all individuals who are subject to a certain body of common or statute law that which is due them under the law, as well as that which is due the community from the members of the society as required by positive law. *Social justice* is the willingness of the individual members of a society or community to contribute whatever is due the community as required by natural law so as to achieve the common good of the society. Thus, justice is the fundamental principle by which every society should be regulated. Since organizations are societies in themselves, as well as parts of larger societies, they definitely should be sensitive to the demands of justice. Finally, the principle of justice is so important to organized groups that even charity, the feeling of benevolence one man has for another, must yield to justice. If justice does not take precedence over charity, then charity begets injustice. For example, a manager may be kind and lenient in judging certain individuals in an organization (charity), but may be the opposite in judging others (injustice). Within any organized groups, as far as relationships between members are concerned, justice is the only right expression of a charitable motive.

Behavioral Aspects

Behavior in organizations is fundamentally human behavior. As such, many concepts developed in the social and behavioral sciences such as economics, psychology, sociology, and anthropology are both relevant and applicable to the management activity of decision-making. This fact has been responsible for many of the new ideas in the study of management in recent years.

ECONOMICS

While the promise of breadth by Alfred Marshall, who defined economics as a study of mankind in the ordinary business of life, has never been realized, many economists have been broadening their outlooks somewhat to include additional variables in their analyses. This is primarily because of the widespread attacks upon the traditional assumption that individuals act rationally to maximize their utility or satisfactions. The lack of realism in the maximization of utility assumption is supported by a number of behavioral factors: (1) the existence of values which are not subject to quantification or objective expression;

(2) the effect of habit patterns; (3) the effect of changes in space, time, and individual proclivities; (4) the influence of social emulation; (5) the effect of emotion; (6) the effect of culture and social institutions; (7) the difficulty or impossibility of most people to understand the mathematical process used by some economists; (8) the effect of physiological processes; (9) the effect of volition or will; and (10) the effect of intuition, impulse, or chance factors. Fortunately, many economists have been attempting to incorporate some of these elements in their concepts and theories to approximate the real world more closely. The consideration of these aspects of behavior in choice or decision situations[9] has brought the economist into an area of major concern not only to the manager but also to the psychologist, the sociologist, and the anthropologist.

PSYCHOLOGY

As a student of human behavior, the psychologist is vitally concerned with the activity of deciding. Since decisions are not made in a vacuum, modern psychology has contributed materially to our knowledge of the conditions and factors which influence the thought processes in action. What happens organically and in the mind of the decision-maker as he attempts to discover and decide upon solutions to problems are questions answered by psychology. The work of psychologists seems to confirm the assertion that individuals operate from a variety of diverse motivations which do not lend themselves to utility maximization. The theories of Sigmund Freud and his followers are only one example of the thought that men are not motivated entirely by rationality in decision-making.

SOCIOLOGY

When a manager makes a decision that affects the behavior of others, he sets in motion social processes of considerable significance to the sociologist in terms of human motives, human group interaction, individual variations in reactions to various social situations, and social change. Moreover, sociologists have

---

[9] See Katona, *Psychological Analysis of Economic Behavior,* as an example of an economist who considers behavioral elements.

accumulated substantial evidence to demonstrate the important influence of social institutions, habit, and tradition upon the decisions made by individuals. The manager cannot escape the fact that his decisions are made in a social framework.

ANTHROPOLOGY

Not to be ignored by the student of decision-making is the influence of a man's culture, ". . . the instrument whereby the individual adjusts to his total setting and gains the means for creative expression."[10] Anthropologists tell us that man differs from animals because he must rely on an artificially fashioned environment—material, spiritual, and social—which becomes a gigantic conditioning apparatus, producing in each succeeding generation its own type of individual. The cultural approach recognizes that the individual's choice of decision process takes place within a cultural matrix: Deciding man is never found in a cultureless state. On the contrary, the prevailing explanation of the effect of culture on the individual emphasizes *primary groups* (relatives, co-workers) who help the individual give meaning to his environment, *language* as the vehicle of communication, *roles* for individuals in various situations, and *status* as the various positions that constitute the structure of a group.[11] Anthropology definitely emphasizes the nonrational or customary aspects of human behavior as much as the rational aspects.

Logical Aspects

Scientists, professional men, and laymen are all tied to logic. We can range only as far as our reason permits. The manipulation of the mathematical and chemical formulae of the scientist, and of the factual and value elements of the professional man and layman, have little meaning unless they are dominated by rigorous logic.

The science of logic has been studied and used since the time of Aristotle. Yet relatively few people seem to be able to reason

[10] Melville J. Herskovits, *Man and His Works: The Science of Cultural Anthropology* (New York: Knopf, 1948), pp. 640–641.

[11] See, for example, C. Addison Hickman and Manford H. Kuhn, *Individuals, Groups, and Economic Behavior* (New York: Dryden, 1956) and Richard T. LaPiere, *A Theory of Social Control* (New York: McGraw-Hill, Inc., 1954)

logically, and even fewer want to accept decisions arrived at logically, unless the decisions happen to coincide with those previously reached on an emotional or volitional basis. Nevertheless, logic can give decision-makers great assistance in solving problems. Without it, the administrator and the supervisor must put their faith in such untrustworthy methods as rule-of-thumb, impulse, or chance.

Decision-making deals with problems, questions, issues, and alternatives. Whether the decision-maker chooses one alternative or another depends very much upon his ability to reason validly. Mastery of logical methodology enables him to get a firm grip on a difficult management or personal problem, for sound logic means sound decisions. Yet ones does not need to be a master of the many technicalities of inductive and deductive methods to use them in making decisions.

PREMISES AND IMPLICATIONS

In addition to philosophy and the behavioral sciences, a decision is derived from premises or antecedents. To doubt this is to say that all decisions of administrators or managers are the arbitrary products of impulse or caprice. A correct and compelling decision is not a simple unsupported assertion; rather, it is a conclusion which is sustained by the premises or antecedents from which it is derived. The value for the decider in understanding premises lies in discovering what decisions may be *validly* drawn from them. As antecedents of decision, premises become what may be called basic raw materials in decision-making. But the implications[12] of premises must not be confused with the decisions based upon the implications. Implication as used here refers to the arrangement of premises and the terms within the premises to determine the validity or falsity of the decisions. The importance of this difference to the decision-maker becomes apparent when it is realized that decisions depend upon implication for their validity.

INDUCTION AND DEDUCTION

Although many decision processes engaged in by the average man mingle inductive and deductive methods, the two are clearly

[12] This and other logical concepts will be briefly discussed in Chapter 7.

distinguishable, and they are the major forms of reasoning. As the word "induction" indicates, to reason inductively is to be led from one position to another until the decision is reached. **Induction is the process of reasoning or inference in which the decision-maker proceeds from individual instances to a more general conclusion.** It is the logic underlying all attempts to solve problems by experience and by experiment. When used conscientiously, the inductive method avoids prejudice and preconceptions, since the honest decision-maker will make every effort not to devise explanations until the data supports them, and he will revise his generalizations when the discovery of new evidence so requires.

Deduction proceeds from the general to the particular. Deductive reasoning begins with general laws, principles, or factual generalizations, and applies them to individual situations. It is the method illustrated by mathematics. The heart of the process is the syllogism, with its well known major and minor premises and conclusion. In deduction, the decision or conclusion is an explicit expression of the implicit relationship contained in the major and minor premises. It is an operation whereby the mind arrives at a decision from a set of logically related premises.

Reasoning about problems and alternative solutions combines building up generalizations from instances (evidence) and applying generalizations to evidence. To make logic work in decision-making, it is necessary to watch for the blending of induction and deduction; the combination is almost indispensable in the solution of many difficult problems.

Quantitative Aspects

That every manager is a decision-maker is hardly denied anywhere or by anybody connected in any way with the field of management, whether as a theoretician or as a practitioner. While no substitutes have been found for sound judgment, a lively interest has recently developed in a great variety of mathematical and statistical tools to be used by management. It must be stated at once, however, that while such quantitative analysis is not a substitute for management, it is a tool of management similar to other tools such as accounting, economics, and budgeting. A certain amount of constructive skepticism is natural in considering the quantitative aspects of decision-making. Like anything else, quantitative analysis can be used improperly and can become a lethal instrument in the wrong hands. Furthermore, there are many significant management problems requiring decisions which simply cannot be given an appropriate quantitative representation, and therefore the manager must rely upon the qualitative approach. Nevertheless, a summary discussion of a few relevant concepts at this point should give the reader some insight into this important tool. For if the manager is to gain the benefits of quantitative analysis, yet protect himself against its misuse, he must acquire some understanding of both its capabilities and its limitations.

ABSTRACTION

In the preceding section on the logical aspects of deciding, induction was defined as a procedure from particular instances. In other words, induction is an attempt to solve problems empirically. But many empirical or real-world problems are enormously complex, so that there is literally an infinite number of instances or facts inherent in many empirical situations. In most cases, if the deciding manager adopted the policy of collecting all the facts he thought he would need before acting, he would never act. Unfortunately, men's minds cannot consider every fact or aspect of every problem found in reality; some aspects of problems must be minimized or even ignored if a decision is to be made at all within the limitations of time and cost. Consequently, the decider must abstract or separate from the empirical situation those factors which he considers to be most relevant to the problem at hand. Abstraction is thus a very necessary step in the solution of many management and personal problems.

MODEL BUILDING

After the manager has selected the critical factors from the real-world situation by abstraction, he then organizes his variables in some logical manner so that they form a model—defined in Chapter 4 as an approximation or representation of reality. After the model has been developed, certain conclusions may be drawn about its behavior by means of deduction. If the relevant variables have been abstracted, and if the deductive conclusions from the abstracted variables are correct, the solution to the model problem should serve as an effective solution for the empirical problem. Errors either in reasoning, in the selection of the wrong variables, or in not selecting enough variables will require that the whole process be repeated. Additional new data are acquired, abstraction takes place again, and a new model is developed, as indicated in Chapter 4.

QUANTITATIVE REPRESENTATION

While models may be physical and verbal, they may also be quantitative or mathematical. If the variables of a model can be given a quantitative or symbolic representation, then there are strong reasons for using such a model. First, an orderly procedure by the investigator is assured in which the opportunity for making assumptions is minimized. Second, quantitative representation or mathematics may result in logical processes in which variables are related and conclusions drawn from premises. The intimate relationship of logical methodology to mathematics should now be apparent to the reader.

Discussion Questions

1. What is the significance to society if top executives made better decisions in the future?
2. What is a decision? What is deciding? What is a judgment? What is a choice?
3. Is a habit a decision? Explain.
4. The statement has been made that deciding is purposive behavior. What does this statement mean?
5. What are the occasions for choice?
6. What is meant by the exception principle?
7. What are the areas where problems requiring choice may be deliberately investigated and researched?
8. Why is decision-making called a pervasive activity of the manager?
9. Why are philosophers concerned with deciding?
10. Morals or ethics are matters for speculative philosophers,

not for practical organization men. Deny or defend this statement.

11. Define the term "ethics."
12. Can the ethical behavior of people be governed by legislation? Why or why not?
13. Does industry have a uniform code of ethics? Should business have such a code?
14. What is prudence? What are the three operations of prudence?
15. What is justice? What is an injustice? Give examples of each drawn from your private daily life and drawn from organizational life.
16. What are the fundamental forms of justice? Define each. Does justice yield to charity or vice-versa? Explain.
17. What fields are included in the behavioral sciences? Why are these important to decision-making?
18. Deciding man is never found in a cultureless state. Discuss the implications of the foregoing statement.
19. Why is some knowledge of logical methodology important to a decision-maker?
20. Why is it necessary to examine the quantitative aspects of deciding? What are the advantages of model building and quantitative representation? When may the mathematical approach not be used?

References

Albers, Henry A., *Organized Executive Action* (New York: Wiley, 1961), Chapter 10.

Ambrose, A., and M. Laserowitz, *Fundamentals of Symbolic Logic* (New York: Rinehart, 1948).

Barnard, Chester I., *The Functions of the Executive* (Cambridge: Harvard University Press, 1938), Chapter 13.

Bellman, Richard, *Dynamic Programming* (Princeton: Princeton University Press, 1957).

Bernhardt, Karl S., *Practical Psychology* (New York: McGraw-Hill, 1945).

Bierman, Harold, Lawrence E. Fouraker, and Robert Jaedicke, *Quantitative Analysis for Business Decisions* (Homewood: Irwin, 1961), Chapter 1.

Blackwell, David, and M. A. Gershick, *Theory of Games and Statistical Decisions* (New York: Wiley, 1954).

Boas, Franz, *Anthropology and Modern Life,* rev. ed. (New York: Norton, 1928).

Bogardus, Emory S., *Fundamentals of Social Psychology,* 4th ed. (New York: Appleton, 1950).

Broehl, Wayne, "Ethics and the Executive: The Small Decisions that Count," *Dun's Review and Modern Industry,* 69, 7 (May, 1957), pp. 45, 122-124.

Broehl, Wayne, "Looking Around: Do Business and Religion Mix?" *Harvard Business Review,* 36, 4 (March-April, 1958), pp. 139-146, 151-152.

Bross, Irwin D. J., *Design for Decision* (New York: Macmillan, 1953), Chapter 1, 2.

Brown, Ray E., *Judgment in Administration* (New York: McGraw-Hill, 1966), Chapter 1.

Campbell, Thomas, "Capitalism and Christianity," *Harvard Business Review,* 35, 4 (July-August, 1957), pp. 37-44.

Cartwright, D., and L. Festinger, "A Quantitative Theory of Decision," *Psychology Review,* Vol. 50 (1943), pp. 595-621.

Churchman, C. W., R. L. Ackoff, and E. L. Arnoff, *Introduction to Operations Research* (New York: Wiley, 1957).

Cohen, Morris R., and Ernest Nagel, *An Introduction to Logical and Scientific Method* (New York: Harcourt Brace, 1934).

Crawford, Robert W., "Operations Research and Its Role in Business Decisions," *Planning for Efficient Production,* Manufacturing Series No. 206 (AMA) (1953), 3-15.

Dean, Joel, *Managerial Economics* (Englewood Cliffs: Prentice-Hall, 1951).

Dempsey, Bernard W., *The Functional Economy* (Englewood Cliffs: Prentice-Hall, 1958).

Dempsey, Bernard, W., *Interest & Usury* (Washington, D.C.: American Council on Public Affairs, 1943).

Dimock, Marshall, "A Philosophy of Administration: Toward Creative Growth," *The Executive,* 2, 7 (December, 1958), pp. 5-9.

Dimock, Marshall, *A Philosophy of Administration* (New York: Harper, 1958) Chapters 7, 15, 17.

Divine, Thomas F., *Interest: An Historical and Analytical Study in Economics and Modern Ethics* (Milwaukee: Marquette University Press, 1959).

Dohrovolsky, S. P., "Depreciation Policies and Investment Decisions," *American Economic Review,* XLI, No. 5 (December, 1951), 906-914.

Drummond, W. F., *Social Justice* (Milwaukee: Bruce, 1955).

Finn, D., "Struggle for Ethics in Public Relations," *Harvard Business Review,* 37, 1 (January-February, 1959), pp. 49-58.

Folsom, Marion B., *Executive Decision-Making* (New York: McGraw-Hill, 1962), Chapter 1.

Gaumnitz, R. K., and O. H. Bronnlei, "Mathematics for Decision-Makers," *Harvard Business Review,* XXXIV (1954), 448-466.

Golomski, W. A., "Linear Programming for Industry," *Marquette Business Review,* Vol. 1, No. 1 (June, 1957), 22-25.

Gore, William J., and James Dyson, ed. *The Making of Decisions* (New York: Free Press, 1964), Part I.

Henderson, Alexander, and Robert Schlaifer, "Mathematical Programming: Better Information for Better Decision-Making," *Harvard Business Review,* Vol. 32, No. 3 (1954), 73-100.

Herskovitz, Melville J., *Man and His Works* (New York: Knopf, 1948).

Higgins, George, "Social Aspects of Automation," *The Executive,* 2, 7 (December, 1958), pp. 9-10.

Johnson, Harold, "An Evaluation of the Social Responsibility of Businessmen Concept," *The Executive,* 1, 2 (July, 1957), pp. 21-22.

Jones, Manley H., *Executive Decision-Making* (Homewood: Irwin, 1957) Chapters 1, 2, 3.

Kimball, George E., "Decision Theory: Operations Research in Management," *Advanced Management,* XVIII, No. 6 (June, 1953), 5-7.

Levitt, T., "The Dangers of Social Responsibility," *Harvard Business Review,* 36, 5 (September-October, 1958), pp. 41-50.

Lindsay, Franklin A., *New Techniques for Management Decision-Making* (New York: McGraw-Hill, 1958), Chapter 1.

MacPhee, E. D., "The Conscience of Business," *The Executive,* 1, 2 (July, 1957), pp. 17-18.

Maier, Norman R. F., *Problem-Solving Discussions and Conferences* (New York: McGraw-Hill, 1963), Chapter 1.

Maier, Norman R. F., and John J. Hayes, *Creative Management* (New York: Wiley, 1962), Chapter 1.

Malinowski, Bronislaw, "Culture as a Determinant of Behavior," *The Scientific Monthly,* XLIII (November, 1936), 440-449.

Maritain, J., *The Person and the Common Good* (New York: Scribner, 1947).

Marquart, D. I., "Group Problem Solving," *Journal of Social Psychology,* Vol. 4 (1955), pp. 103-113.

Mikanovich, C. S., and J. B. Schuyler, *Current Social Problems,* (Milwaukee: Bruce, 1950).

Miller, David W., and Martin K. Starr, *Executive Decisions and Operations Research* (Englewood Cliffs: Prentice-Hall, 1960), Chapters 1, 2.

Miltner, Charles C., *The Elements of Ethics,* 2nd rev. ed. (New York: Macmillan, 1936), Parts I, II.

Morell, R. W., "What Is a Decision?" *Hospital Progress,* Vol. 39, No. 2, February, 1958.

Morell, R. W., "Operations Research in Decision-Making," *Marquette Business Review,* II, No. 5 (December, 1950), 22.

Newman, William H., and Charles E. Summer, Jr., *The Process of Management* (Englewood Cliffs: Prentice-Hall, 1961), Chapter 12.

Nordling, Rolf, "Social Responsibilities of Today's Industrial Leaders," *Advanced Management,* XXII, 4 (April, 1957), pp. 18-22.

Northrop, F. S. C., *The Logic of the Sciences and the Humanities* (New York: Macmillan, 1947).

Ohmann, O. A. "Search for a Managerial Philosophy," *Harvard Business Review,* 35, 5 (September-October, 1957), pp. 41-51.

Randall, Clarence B., "For a New Code of Business Ethics," *New York Times Magazine,* April 8, 1962, p. 24ff.

Robinson, Claude, *Understanding Profits* (Princeton: Van Nostrand, 1961), Chapter 13.

Ruegg, Fred F., "Ethical Responsibility of Management," *Advanced Management,* February, 1962, p. 5ff.

Seleckman, Benjamin, "Cynicism and Managerial Morality," *Harvard Business Review,* 36, 5 (September-October, 1958), pp. 61-71.

Seleckman, Benjamin, *A Moral Philosophy for Management* (New York: McGraw-Hill, 1959), Chapter 1, 10; Parts IV, VI.

Sherif, Muzafer, *An Outline of Social Psychology* (New York: Harper, 1948).

Shubik, Marin, "The Uses of Game Theory in Management Science," *Management Science,* Vol. 2 (1955), 40-54.

Simon, Herbert A., *The New Science of Management Decision* (New York: Harper, 1960), Chapter 1.

Smith, R. A., "The Incredible Electrical Conspiracy," *Fortune,* April, 1961, p. 132ff; May, 1961, pp. 161ff.

Stover, Carl, "Changing Patterns in the Philosophy of Management," *The Executive,* 2, 4 (September, 1958), pp. 9-10.

Sutherland, E., "White Collar Criminality," *American Sociological Review,* February, 1940, 1ff.

Tannenbaum, Robert, and Fred Massarick, "Participation by Subordinates in the Managerial Decision-Making Process," *Canadian Journal of Economics and Political Science,* XVI, August, 1950, pp. 408-418.

Terry, George R., *Principles of Management,* 3rd ed. (Homewood: Irwin, 1960), Chapter 3.

Vance, Stanley, *Industrial Administration* (New York: McGraw-Hill, 1959), Chapter 7.

Worthy, James, "Freedom within American Enterprise," *Advanced Management,* XIX, 6 (June, 1954), pp. 5-8.

Worthy, James, "Religion and Its Role in the World of Business," *The Journal of Business,* XXXI, 4 (October, 1958), pp. 293-303.

Chapter 6. Behavioral Factors in Management

Psychological Factors in Management
  Perception
    Determinants of Perception
    Perception and Interpersonal Relations
    Conclusions
  Emotions
    Emotional Stimulation and Decision-Making
    Frustration
    Anxiety
    Conflict
  Values and Attitudes
  Habits
  Physical Condition

Social-Anthropological Factors in Management
  Culture and Management
  Culture and Leadership
    Decisiveness
    Physical and Constitutional Factors
    Personality
    Emotional Stability
    Initiative
    Integrity
    Diplomacy
  Participation and Group Dynamics

Conclusions

Discussion Questions

References

Chapter 6

Behavioral Factors in Management

> We have to get closer up before we can make a good decision,
> and it calls for great courage to go up to a problem
> instead of waiting for it to come to us.—CHARLES P. CURTIS

Although it is largely by making decisions that man has become
master of this planet, decision-making is a burdensome task
which requires considerable mental effort and which should not
be approached aimlessly. Because of this and because a decision
is so significantly affected by the individual's awareness and
knowledge of the decision-making process and the various elements involved in this process, it is necessary that some of these
elements be examined at length in this and in subsequent
chapters. While the point of departure of this analysis could be
anywhere, it seems to me that, since organizational behavior is
basically human behavior, it should begin with a discussion of
man as a behavioral animal, that is, as a psychological being
behaving and deciding within some culture.

PSYCHOLOGICAL FACTORS IN MANAGEMENT

During the twentieth century the word "psychology" has virtually become a household term. Not only do misinformed people use it but they seem to enjoy using it in a carefree manner.
The use of the term "psychological" here is an attempt to draw
attention to the existence of certain mental and physical factors
which act as *deterrents to rational choice*. These subjective factors
militate against the decision-maker, often without his being
aware of them, when he is attempting to arrive at decisions.
Factors such as perception, emotion, values, habit, and physical
condition influence decision-making to a far greater extent than

most people are willing to admit. The result is that many people in and out of management frequently make unfortunate decisions for which they pay heavily in terms of money, misery, and failure. To fully appreciate how to make valid and true decisions one must be aware of these subjective factors and understand how they operate. Thus, it is the purpose of this inquiry to examine and analyze some of the factors which frequently keep us from making good decisions.

Perception

Perhaps a useful way to begin an analysis of the psychological factors in decision-making is to start at the beginning, with the initial cognitive (knowing) process. That process is **perception —a cognitive process involving the apprehension of organized wholes at the sensory level.**[1] That is, perception is a knowing function of the sensuous order by which the individual mentally takes hold of organized wholes. By "organized wholes" we mean that although our sense organs constantly receive stimuli, we do not normally experience external objects as a chaos of unrelated sights, sounds, tastes, or smells. On the contrary, the normal individual, for example, perceives a room as filled with furniture and people. Moreover, he may observe that the room is too hot or too cold, or that the television is too loud, or that the room is crowded. Thus, he has perceptually organized the separate elements in the room into some kind of an organized whole.

DETERMINANTS OF PERCEPTION

Recent behavioral science research has led us away from the more mechanical approach to perception to what may now be called "the new look in perception."[2] We now know that perception is not merely an objective or mechanical "stimulus-response" process. On the contrary, our basic needs (physical, social, ego), values, attitudes, cultural background, stresses, as-

[1] F. L. Harmon, *Principles of Psychology*, rev. ed. (Milwaukee: Bruce, 1951), p. 149.

[2] See "Social Psychology and Perception" in E. Maccoby, T. Newcomb, and E. Hartley, ed., *Readings in Social Psychology*, 3rd ed. (New York: Holt, 1958), and Chapters 1, 2, 3 of T. W. Costello and S. S. Zalkind, *Psychology in Administration* (Englewood Cliffs: Prentice-Hall, 1963), pp. 6-54.

sumptions, concepts, education, experience, religion, language, social conventions and the like all affect our perceptions. All these factors may cause our perceptions to be distorted, selected, and often cause us to use defense mechanisms. In other words, perception, which is based on sensory experience and which initiates thinking, is significantly influenced by one or more of the elements mentioned above. Consequently, refined sense perception is not merely the sensory experience of sight or touch, but is also the product of our entire conceptual framework.

PERCEPTION AND INTERPERSONAL RELATIONS

Forming impressions of others is indeed one of the most frequent and most important perceptions the individual makes. Most of us have been guilty of stereotyping (assigning certain qualities to people because of group membership, such as assuming that accountants are conservative), of using physical traits as the basis for judgment (some people like redheads), of using a general impression to evaluate specific traits (thinking that someone who smiles is sincere), or permitting our emotions to distort our perceptions of others.

If we seriously desire better interpersonal relations, we should try to know ourselves and our own characteristics. This is quite necessary when we realize that we then perceive the ways others are similar to us more accurately. Thus, our own characteristics affect those we see in others. In addition, we respond to a relationship—for example, a subordinate's response to a superior will be significantly affected by the fact that the subordinate is responding to his boss, and the same stimulus will evoke quite a different response from an associate or a subordinate.

CONCLUSIONS

We can say of our perceptions that no one sees the real world precisely as we do. We are products of our experience and we are not stereotypes of each other. Moreover, the manager should become aware of the perceptual process, and should seek reliable evidence before making arbitrary judgments, especially about people. Finally, he should permit modifications of his own perceptions and be able to shift his position as in time we learn more about objects and people.

Emotions

It is almost universally recognized by psychologists and laymen that emotional experiences have a significant effect on an individual's behavior. Everyday experiences show how feelings and emotions affect the thought processes; how, for example, anger, fear, or jealousy can distort the mental process of making decisions. It therefore is natural to ask, "What is emotion?" **Emotion is a complex state of mental excitement which follows perception**[3] **of an exciting object or situation and leads to certain changes in bodily functions and behavior.**[4] In other words, emotion is an inner feeling or disturbance which leads to some kind of physical reaction. Examples of such reactions are the physiological responses which usually accompany emotional stimulation. Under great fear, for instance, the adrenal gland secretes a hormone called adrenin into the bloodstream. Under this influence the heartbeat increases, the blood pressure rises, respiration is stepped up, digestion slows or stops, the nervous system is alerted for immediate action, the liver releases stored-up sugar into the blood, and the chemical composition of the blood changes so the blood will clot more readily if necessary. In short, the body prepares itself for whatever action ("fight or flight") may be required. The pattern of physiological changes, of course, varies according to the particular emotion involved (the pattern would be quite different for grief or despair), and to the intensity of the individual's feelings with respect to his perception of the situation. Thus, we see that emotions are indispensable to an individual's adjustment to a situation.

EMOTIONAL STIMULATION AND DECISION-MAKING

In decision-making situations, mild emotional stimulation may initially have a tonic effect on the mind by increasing mental alertness and mental endurance. Very soon thereafter, however, even the mildest emotion seems to hamper rational thought in any situation requiring objectivity. Strong emotions like anger and fear are about as useful to rational decision-making as

[3] The reader should note the use of the word "perception" in Harmon's definition of emotion. It should now be clear why perception preceded emotion in our discussion. Emotion is, at least in part, a function of perception.

[4] Harmon, *Principles of Psychology*, p. 545.

lighted matches in a dynamite factory. Such emotions inhibit sound decision-making in at least three ways. First, whenever the decision-maker judges an uncertain situation as problematic, he may become so concerned with the threat and the defensive thoughts (fear) that he finds it difficult to concentrate on the problem. It seems as though fear brings on the things we fear. Second, fear causes the physiological effect of redistribution of the blood supply, reducing the nourishment to the brain, so that an individual may function less effectively. Third, emotions reduce the control of thought over decision-making. While under strong emotional tension, we have an urge to decide something at once, even if it is unwise, rather than wait until we can reflectively consider the situation. For example, the physical act of "poking" another man on the jaw or the verbal act of "getting mad" at another are emotional acts. Such acts are usually accompanied by the decision to act immediately despite the fact that they are clearly unwise. But rational decisions require thought and reflection, not dilated pupils; we realize that the effect of such physiological changes makes rational decision-making much more difficult, if not impossible.

FRUSTRATION

The decision-maker cannot hope to protect himself completely from psychological adversity. Emotional stress and strain may well lead to frustration, anxiety, and conflict. A brief inquiry into such emotional experiences may help a manager to better understand himself and others in the decision-making process.

"Frustration" as an emotional experience is essentially the result of past or present painful feelings (need denial).[5] It is the term which describes an interference with an individual's direct progress toward a goal as well as describing a state of mind. Whereas frustration is the response to an existing event, **anxiety is the response to the threat of such an event.**[6] Thus, frustration is a response to a past or present event, while anxiety refers to a possible future painful event.

The emotional experiences or painful feelings of need denial or goal nonrealization must have causes. These causes are

[5] Costello and Zalkind, *Psychology in Administration,* p. 150.
[6] *Ibid.*

stressors—defined as disturbances or strains in the environment.[7]
Stressors include obstacles in the way of achieving goals; unreasonable demands; poor and taxing work conditions; noise and uncomfortable temperatures; uncertain roles to be played by a manager; and injustices and errors of superiors, subordinates, and associates. Such stressors can quickly turn a satisfied individual into a frustrated one. And a frustrated individual can be a troubled individual who finds it difficult to buckle down and concentrate on a problem requiring a decision.

Responses of individuals to frustration vary from optimism to some form of aggressive behavior and/or defense mechanism. The extent of one's aggression is affected by the degree of interference he experiences as well as by the number of interferences preceding frustration. A minor interference or irritation such as an associate's harmless teasing or a child's naughtiness or crying, when a person is fatigued may well result in aggressive behavior which is out of proportion to the event that triggered it.

Defense mechanisms may also serve an important function for the frustrated individual. "When used moderately, defense mechanisms suggest adjustive difficulties an emotionally healthy person is having; when they dominate behavior to the exclusion of more effective behavior, they can constitute a serious personality problem."[8] Figure 6-1 presents a listing of the more common defense mechanisms with examples.

ANXIETY

Someone once said that neurosis is the price we pay for civilization. While this may be subject to some debate, living totally without anxiety in a complex and competitive period like the present would be unrealistic and even irresponsible, particularly towards one's duties as a breadwinner and as a citizen. Yet, most people devote a great deal of energy to the avoidance of more anxiety and to the reduction of whatever anxiety they already have. Why? Probably because they associate anxiety with worry and defense mechanisms and, in the extreme, with emotional maladjustment. Actually, moderate anxiety can raise the level of aspiration of an individual and help him mobilize increased

[7] *Ibid.*, p. 128.   [8] *Ibid.*, p. 148.

Adjustive Reactions	Psychological Process	Illustration
Compensation	Individual devotes himself to a pursuit with increased vigor to make up for some feeling of real or imagined inadequacy	Zealous, hard-working president of the Twenty-five Year Club who has never advanced very far in the company hierarchy
Conversion	Emotional conflicts are expressed in muscular, sensory, or bodily symptoms of disability, malfunctioning, or pain	A disabling headache keeping a staff member off the job, the day after a cherished project has been rejected
Displacement	Re-directing pent-up emotions toward persons, ideas, or objects other than the primary source of the emotion	Roughly rejecting a simple request from a subordinate after receiving a rebuff from the boss
Fantasy	Day-dreaming or other forms of imaginative activity provide an escape from reality and imagined satisfactions	An employee's day-dream of the day in the staff meeting when he corrects the boss' mistakes and is publicly acknowledged as the real leader of the industry
Identification	Individual enhances his self-esteem by patterning his own behavior after another's, frequently also internalizing the values and beliefs of the other; also vicariously sharing the glories of suffering in the reversals of other individuals or groups	The "assistant-to" who takes on the vocabulary, mannerisms, or even pomposity of his vice-presidential boss
Negativism	Active or passive resistance, operating unconsciously	The manager who, having been unsuccessful in getting out of a committee assignment, picks apart every suggestion that anyone makes in the meetings
Projection	Individual protects himself from awareness of his own undesirable traits or unacceptable feelings by attributing them to others	Unsuccessful person who, deep down, would like to block the rise of others in the organization and who continually feels that others are out to "get him"
Rationalization	Justifying inconsistent or undesirable behavior, beliefs, statements and motivations by providing acceptable explanations for them	Padding the expense account because "everybody does it"

Reaction-Formation	Urges not acceptable to consciousness are repressed and in their stead opposite attitudes or modes of behavior are expressed with considerable force	Employee who has not been promoted who overdoes the defense of his boss, vigorously upholding the company's policies
Regression	Individual returns to an earlier and less mature level of adjustment in the face of frustration	A manager having been blocked in some administrative pursuit busies himself with clerical duties or technical details, more appropriate for his subordinates
Repression	Completely excluding from consciousness impulses, experiences, and feelings which are psychologically disturbing because they arouse a sense of guilt or anxiety	A subordinate "forgetting" to tell his boss the circumstances of an embarrassing situation
Fixation	Maintaining a persistent nonadjustive reaction even though all the cues indicate the behavior will not cope with the problems	Persisting in carrying out an operational procedure long since declared by management to be uneconomical as a protest because the employee's opinion wasn't asked
Resignation, Apathy, and Boredom	Breaking psychological contact with the environment, withholding any sense of emotional or personal involvement	Employee who, receiving no reward, praise, or encouragement, no longer cares whether or not he does a good job
Flight or Withdrawal	Leaving the field in which frustration, anxiety, or conflict is experienced, either physically or psychologically	The salesman's big order falls through and he takes the rest of the day off; constant rebuff or rejection by superiors and colleagues, pushes an older worker toward being a loner and ignoring what friendly gestures are made

FIGURE 6-1. **Adjustive reactions to frustration, conflict, and anxiety.** Source: Timothy W. Costello and Sheldon S. Zalkind, *Psychology in Administration: A Research Orientation*, © 1963. Reprinted by permission of Prentice-Hall, Inc., Englewood Cliffs, N.J.

energy to achieve higher goals. This constructive use of anxiety is exemplified by those who have worked productively while experiencing anxiety, with the result that they have been able to meet present and future anxiety experiences with less trepidation.

The nature of anxiety can perhaps be better understood if we return for a moment to its definition. In the preceding section, anxiety was defined as the response to the threat of a frustrating future event. The key to the understanding of the essence of anxiety lies in the answer to the question, *"What is threatened in the experience which produces anxiety?"* The threat is to something in the core of the personality. As defined by Rollo May, **"Anxiety is the apprehension cued off by a threat to some value which the individual holds essential to his existence as a personality."**[9] Examples of threats include death, love of another person, loss of freedom, patriotism, success, and the like. An individual experiences fear because he has developed a security pattern over a period of time; he experiences anxiety because the security pattern itself is being threatened.

While it is a valid generalization to say that moderate anxiety can help a manager to reach a higher level of productivity, severe anxiety may be debilitative; that is, it may have a negative effect on the decision-maker's behavior. A more precise example of this statement is shown in Figure 6-2.

CONFLICT

In addition to frustration and anxiety, another response to stress is conflict—**"an internal state in which the individual is being pulled in opposite directions by forces within himself."**[10] It would seem that the person experiencing conflict is in what might be called a "state of emotional disequilibrium."

One form of conflict useful for the decision-maker is what psychologists call "cognitive dissonance." The word "cognitive" has already been alluded to earlier as meaning knowing; the term "dissonance" is synonymous with inconsistent, contradictory, and incongruous. Accordingly, **"cognitive dissonance" in-**

[9] *Ibid.*, pp. 151-152. Excerpted from Rollo May, *The Meaning of Anxiety* (New York: Ronald, 1950), Chapter 6.
[10] Costello and Zalkind, p. 168.

Slight Anxiety	Moderate Anxiety	Severe Anxiety
General alerting	Less spontaneity	Organization of behavior breaks down
Increased sensitivity to outside events	Rigidity, reliance on "safe" habitual responses	Inability to distinguish between safe and harmful stimuli
Physiological mobilization	Reduced ability to improvise	Stereotyped, unadaptive, random-appearing patterns
Effective integration of behavior	More effort needed to maintain adequate behavior	Irritability, distractability
Increase in ability for productive behavior	Narrowing and distortion of perception	Impaired learning, thinking

FIGURE 6-2. **Effects of anxiety.** These generalizations are drawn from many studies including Cannon, 1939; Liddell, 1944; Combs, 1952; Ausubel and others, 1954; Basowitz and others, 1955. Source: Timothy W. Costello and Sheldon S. Zalkind, *Psychology in Administration: A Research Orientation,* © 1963. Reprinted by permission of Prentice-Hall, Inc., Englewood Cliffs, N.J.

dicates the existence of incompatible beliefs or attitudes held simultaneously by the individual.

Cognitive dissonance may be conscious or unconscious. For example, most of the readers who are smokers know by now that it is a habit that may lead to lung cancer. The smoker knows what the reports say, and can stop smoking if this knowledge makes him consciously uncomfortable; or he can ignore this knowledge so that it becomes subconscious. The thought about cancer may reappear from time to time in the smoker's consciousness, causing him to ridicule the research findings or to rationalize his smoking, thereby distorting his knowledge and forcing it into the subconscious once again.

Values and Attitudes

Sigmund Freud has been paraphrased as saying that the only touch many people have with reality is the long arm of the job. If we reflect for a moment on this, and at the same time think of the fact that in organizational life one is provided with goals by the organization—a form of purposive behavior—as well as the need for making decisions to achieve these goals, we can quickly see some merit in Freud's statement. But even on the job one has to face and to attempt to mitigate whenever possible the psychological factors that are deterrents to rational choice. We have examined the two very important psychological factors of perception and emotion, but there are others:

Attitude is the predisposition of the individual to evaluate some symbol or object or aspect of his world in a favorable or unfavorable manner. Opinion is the verbal expression of an attitude . . . When specific attitudes are organized into a hierarchical structure, they comprise *value systems*.[11]

All of us have gradually built up over the years a structure of attitudes and values from accumulated experiences and varying backgrounds. We have been subjected to cultural influences—customs, habits, traditions, group memberships in religious, educational, and socioeconomic institutions, the family, peer groups, and various work experiences. Thus, our attitude formation and the build-up of the value system is quite personal, and different from those of other individuals.

In the management process, the manager uses attitudes and values as premises or parts of premises in the countless decisions called for in his day-to-day activities. Actually, in decision-making a manager must use such elements because virtually every decision contains some degree of value characteristics. Moreover, even if we assume that we are dealing with purely factual elements in decision-making, it is continually necessary to choose factual elements whose truth or falsity cannot be determined with certainty even with the data, cost, and time available for reaching the decision. The serious difficulty with attitudes and value measures is that most of us tend to think of our own attitudes and value standards as objective; we frequently assume that everyone else uses the same attitudes and value scale as we do when nobody has precisely the same scale of values however similar the total experience may be. Nevertheless, value elements are indispensable to the decision-maker because factual elements are often not available while he is anticipating favorable or unfavorable consequences of alternatives, dealing with imponderables, or making decisions based upon inadequate information. Yet

[11] *Ibid.*, p. 253.

the manager should be aware that he is constantly using his own attitudes and value elements and that he should use them with caution.

Habits

Many writers such as Katona and Barnard emphasize the distinction between genuine decision and habit (see Chapter 5). The position usually taken by the experts is that the psychological process in habitual behavior is different from that found in the more conscious or rational behavior called "decision." This does not mean that habits in themselves are undesirable. On the contrary, they are indispensable to everyday living because they represent acts repeated without conscious thought. It is probably safe to say that most individuals rise in the morning, wash, dress, eat, work, play, sleep, and perform the innumerable activities of the day in patterns which they have learned and which have become habit patterns. However, it must be kept in mind that uniform habits of responding to various problematic situations can be harmful to the decision-maker. The tendency of an individual to persist in a particular method of attack on a problem, even when it is unsuccessful, is one of the major drawbacks of habits. A habit becomes a handicap when it is not bringing success. One antidote is the use of failure as a signal for a new approach or a new method. It is a good idea to test even successful approaches or methods from time to time by setting up rival alternatives.

Physical Condition

Most of us know that the quality of our thought processes is affected by illness, fatigue, and physical discomfort. The close interrelationship between body and mind is shown in many ways. We have all observed, for example, the effects of alcohol on otherwise well behaved people. Certain endocrine products in the bloodstream affect what one remembers or imagines by lowering or raising the thresholds of perception. The body-mind relationship is so close that many decision-makers have learned through experience that it is wise to maintain good health and, when possible, to postpone making important decisions while tired, sleepy, ill, or under medication. Valid and wise decisions are more likely to be the products of a sound mind at work in a sound body.

SOCIAL-ANTHROPOLOGICAL FACTORS IN MANAGEMENT

Every community develops some system to regulate its own operations. This "system" aspect of culture is shown in Figure 6-3, from which we can see that the relationship between the

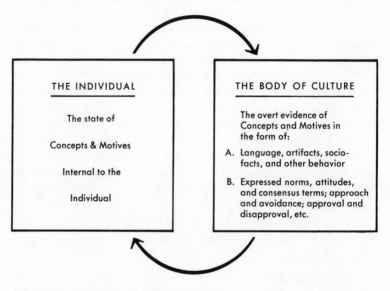

FIGURE 6-3. **The system of culture.** Source: Alfred Kuhn, *The Study of Society* (Homewood: Irwin, 1963), p. 206.

individual and culture is something of a chicken-egg situation. The body of culture is the environment into which the individual is born and from which he learns many things about the world around him. The things he learns influence the kind of overt response he gives to a stimulus. Accordingly, individuals say hello and goodbye, wear similar clothes, eat similar foods, speak the language of their community, and approve and disapprove of many similar things. On the other hand, the culture is a matrix which is influenced and shaped by individuals because their behavior is part of the culture.

Culture and Management

Once the pervasiveness of the cultural dimension is recognized, economic activity and managerial behavior must be perceived as falling under its constraints.[12] The sociocultural approach recognizes that the economic process takes place within a cultural matrix: The manager is never found making decisions in a vacuum or cultureless state. As a matter of fact, management is one subculture (one of many subcultures which make up the total culture) with its own groups, roles, status, and language. Management as a subculture is a mosaic of sub-subcultures which take different forms, depending on how the "genus" management is sliced into "species."[13] Consequently, there are large corporations, small businesses, department stores, discount houses, hospitals, railroads, other service firms, and so forth. In each case, there are distinct patterns which develop in organizations, types of leaders, choice of facts on which decisions are made, how decisions are made, management systems, accounting systems, advertising programs, status symbols, budgeting, styles of leadership and followership, the structuring of power, and politics and administrative strategies. For example, it is obvious that the kind of organization required for a prison, in which control is a life-and-death matter, must differ markedly from that required in a newspaper office, where individual initiative and creativity remain important.[14] Thus, we see that the varying nature of the work to be done as well as a variety of environmental factors help to build up the institutional management subculture.

Culture and Leadership

A leader in the Western culture is a person who attempts to influence others. The ability to influence subordinates, asso-

---

[12] J. W. McGuire, ed., *Interdisciplinary Studies in Business Behavior* (Cincinnati: South-Western, 1962), p. 194.

[13] *Ibid.*, p. 201.

[14] John M. Pfiffner and F. Sherwood, *Administrative Organization* (Englewood Cliffs: Prentice-Hall, 1960), p. 266.

ciates, and superiors seems basic to the leadership function. But there is more to leadership than persuasion. This brings up a most important question: What are the essential qualities of successful leadership?

The qualities necessary for effective leadership are those which contribute most to effective action by individuals and by group members. Although many people list a variety of leadership qualities, with no consistent pattern emerging, the following list represents what I believe is essential to effective managerial behavior in the United States culture.

DECISIVENESS

This is the ability to definitively make a decision, a judgment, when one is called for. Included is the ability to detect and verbalize problems to prepare them for analysis; to collect or have collected relevant factual materials; to propose creative and relevant alternatives; to verify; and to implement decisions. Decisiveness includes not only "logical processes," which involve thinking which can be expressed in words or symbols—that is, reasoning; but also "nonlogical processes" which may be incapable of being expressed in words or symbols and which may be called "intuition."[15]

PHYSICAL AND CONSTITUTIONAL FACTORS

These factors include physical appearance, dress, personality, voice, height, weight, physique, health, and energy. It has often been said that a successful person should also be superior in appearance if he expects people to follow him. An intelligent leader who is dressed in shabby clothes and is greatly overweight may experience some difficulties in mobilizing followers in many of today's large progressive corporations in which the "Ivy League look" is emulated.

PERSONALITY

The term "personality" is a generic term which can include almost all characteristics of an individual. For this discussion,

[15] It may be of interest to note here that in other cultures, such as in parts of the Orient and South America, circumlocution is involved more in decision-making than in the United States, often to the dismay of American businessmen operating in foreign countries.

I mean a pleasing personality with which to promote goodwill within an organization. An individual must possess the ability to attract people and inspire their confidence and loyalty; he should be genial, enthusiastic, cheerful, verbal and expressive, persuasive, and sociable.

EMOTIONAL STABILITY

Display of bad temperament, while unfortunate for anybody, becomes inexcusable when displayed by a leader. A leader should not express nervous irritability even though he will undoubtedly experience frustration, anxiety, and internal conflict as a normal phenomenon of day-to-day administration. He must be able to bounce back so that his emotional involvement never becomes excessive.

INITIATIVE

Those who are destined for prominence in leadership are self starters. We all make mistakes, but leaders push on making the most of their capabilities and judgment.

INTEGRITY

An individual who aspires to be a leader cannot treat others differently from the way he would like to be treated. He must be honest, sincere, and possess an inordinate sensitivity to the principle of justice. He should be willing to hear all sides of every question and be reluctant to practice favoritism.

DIPLOMACY

Being a leader in an organization probably requires more tact and discretion in handling people than does leadership in other professions. Since managers get things done by directing other people, the importance of being tactful and diplomatic is clear. It may be necessary for a leader to support his ideas against opposition, but he must do so with the least disturbance to the morale of the individual or group involved. He must constantly remind himself of the attitudes of others, the need for motivation of subordinates, the feelings and emotions of others, the basic needs and desires of others—in short, his study of "human behavior" is neverending if he is to survive as a leader.

Participation and Group Dynamics

Much more significant than the traitist theory of leadership is the fact that the manager cannot escape the reality that, whatever his personal traits may be, his decisions are made in a social framework. Indeed, what makes man human is the fundamental fact that he "lives" with other people in small groups and organizations. Although organization groups are forced-choice groups—the members have not chosen one another, as in the family—they do provide frequency of personal contact and opportunities for participation and shared values.

Although managerial attitudes differ with respect to **"participation," defined as "an individual's mental and emotional involvement in a group situation that encourages him to contribute to group goals and to share responsibility for them,"**[16] more managers are beginning to recognize that subordinates have the ability to think, to come up with new ideas, and to initiate new ways of doing things. The development of participation began with the late Elton Mayo's research at the Hawthorne Works in the 1930's. He showed that a group is more productive and satisfied when its members perceive that they are participatively involved. This interpretation was expanded further by Likert and Argyris in their "employee-oriented supervisor" concepts, and by McGregor's popular "Theory Y" (see Chapters 3 and 4). Moreover, sophisticated managers are not unaware of the theories of leadership discussed by researchers such as Mayo, Likert, Argyris, and McGregor. For instance, Crawford H. Greenewalt, former president of DuPont, presents two methods for motivating superior performance: (1) employee-centered supervision; (2) financial compensation. Ralph J. Cordiner, former president of General Electric, stresses two other techniques: (1) clear delineation of responsibilities; (2) leadership by persuasion. Note that both Cordiner and Greenewalt list as one of their methods one of the leadership theories expounded by the social researchers. Finally, Thomas J. Watson, Jr., chairman of IBM, goes beyond the claims of social researchers such as McGregor and Argyris,

---

[16] Keith Davis, "The Case for Participative Management," in *Human Relations in Management,* 2nd ed. edited by I. L. Huneryager and S. G. Heckmann (Cincinnati: South-Western, 1967), p. 617.

and attributes long-term organizational success to a firm's *"beliefs"* upon which it premises all its policies and actions.[17] The most important belief is "respect for the individual," according to Watson. This respect means that the individual's complaints will be heard without fear of employment termination. His theory is that when the individual is freed of the anxieties associated with employment, he will spontaneously do his best on the job.

Finally, some of the advantages of participation include: (1) use of positive motivation; (2) ego satisfaction; (3) greater decision-making cooperation; (4) increased productivity and creativity; (5) reduction of interpersonal conflict; (6) reduction in labor turnover; (7) greater readiness to accept change. On the other hand, some of the limitations of participation include: (1) the possibility of getting lost in participation procedures such as proliferation of committees; (2) participation requires time; (3) financial cost may exceed values attained; (4) poor choice of subordinates may make participation difficult—for example, some may be unable to communicate effectively. In summary, we can say that people become more responsible and creative, and even exhibit greater degrees of initiative, when given the opportunity to share in decisions as participants in groups, especially when the group has been created by very careful selection of its leader and members.

CONCLUSIONS

The decision-maker who seeks greater objectivity and rationality in management and decision-making should cultivate an awareness of the internal and external forces, such as perception, emotion, attitudes and values, habits, physical condition, and social and cultural factors, while he is engaged in making managerial decisions. An awareness of these factors is the first step toward their control. Whatever factors influence our decisions and actions unconsciously will then influence them consciously. This progress alone can be of immeasurable benefit in raising the rational level of one's managerial behavior.

[17] Saul W. Gellerman, *The Management of Human Relations* (New York: Holt, 1966), pp. 52-58.

Discussion Questions

1. What is perception? What are its determinants?
2. What is emotion? How does emotion affect decision-making?
3. Distinguish between frustration, anxiety, and conflict.
4. What are defense mechanisms?
5. Define the following terms: cognitive dissonance, attitude, values, habits.
6. How is one's physical condition related to decision-making?
7. What is "culture"?
8. What is the "system" aspect of culture?
9. What is meant by the phrase "management is a subculture"?
10. What is "leadership"?
11. List and discuss the characteristics of leadership.
12. What is meant by "participation"?
13. What are the advantages of participation?
14. What are the limitations of participation?
15. How may the awareness of the psychological and social-anthropological factors in management affect one's managerial behavior? Explain.
16. Is management unaware of the problems discussed by social researchers? Explain.
17. Compare the social researchers' theories of leadership to the theories expounded by some sophisticated management practitioners. What do we find?
18. Is the traitist theory of leadership of any value? Explain.
19. Compare the traitist theory of leadership to the other theories of leadership.
20. What is the first step toward the control of the nonrational factors in management?

References

Costello, T. W., and S. S. Zalkind, *Psychology in Administration* (Englewood Cliffs: Prentice-Hall, 1963), Part 3.

Davis, Keith, "The Case for Participative Management," in *Hu-*

man *Relations in Management,* 2nd ed. edited by I. L. Huneryager and S. G. Heckmann (Cincinnati: South-Western, 1967).

Harmon, Francis L., *Principles of Psychology,* rev. ed. (Milwaukee: Bruce, 1961), Chapters 6, 7.

Huneryager, I. L., and S. G. Heckmann, *Human Relations in Management,* 2nd ed. (Cincinnati: South-Western, 1967), Part 7.

Kuhn, Alfred, *The Study of Society* (Homewood: Irwin, 1963). Chapter 12.

Maccoby, E., T. Newcomb, and E. Hartley, ed., "Social Psychology and Perception" in *Readings in Social Psychology,* 3rd ed. (New York: Holt, 1958).

May, Rollo, *The Meaning of Anxiety* (New York: Ronald, 1950), Chapter 6.

McGuire, J. W., ed., *Interdisciplinary Studies in Business Behavior* (Cincinnati: South-Western, 1962), Chapter 11.

Pfiffner, John M., and F. Sherwood, *Administrative Organization* (Englewood Cliffs: Prentice-Hall, 1960), Chapters 3, 14.

Vinacke, W. E., *The Psychology of Thinking* (New York: McGraw-Hill, 1952), Chapters 6, 9.

Chapter 7. Judgment and Inference

Chapter 7

Judgment and Inference

"It is by education, I learn to do by choice,
what other men do by the constraint of fear."—ARISTOTLE

In the preceding chapter, some of the psychological and social-anthropological factors in management were examined to bring to a conscious level some of the factors that are usually unconscious. But there are other factors influencing decision-making—the thought processes of judgment and inference, for instance. As with any behavioral process, thinking is subject to the influence of perceptual, emotional, attitudinal, habitual, physiological, cultural and social elements. In addition, individual differences in thinking result from differences in intellectual capacity, intelligence, conception, judgment, and inference.

INTELLECT AND INTELLIGENCE

Whereas perception is the initial cognitive or knowing process which stimulates the thought process, **the intellect is that quality of mind which enables the individual to think and thus to acquire and retain knowledge.**[1] Intellect "is the ability to understand the inner nature of things as well as the relationships existing among them; the capacity to develop and deal with abstractions, to apprehend causes as such, and to predict effects."[2] **Intelligence,** on the other hand, **is the product of the intellect—** that is, intelligence is what remains after the intellect has acted upon facts and things. Intelligence represents stored-up

---

[1] For more extended discussions of these matters see Francis L. Harmon, *Principles of Psychology,* rev. ed. (Milwaukee, Bruce, 1951), Chapter 12, and Ray E. Brown, *Judgment in Administration* (New York: McGraw-Hill, 1966), Chapter 1.

[2] Harmon, *Principles of Psychology,* p. 356.

knowledge, and is what is measured by intelligence tests. The difference between intellect and intelligence, then, is that intellect refers to an ability of an individual while intelligence refers to the manifestations of that ability. For example, a genius and an idiot do not differ because one has no intellect and the other does; on the contrary, both the genius and the idiot have an intellect—the difference is that the intellect of the genius is able to manifest itself (intelligence) , whereas the intellect of the idiot is prevented from doing so because of a deficient physiological mechanism.[3]

This brings us to another term, intellectual activity, which is closely associated and sometimes confused with the terms intellect and intelligence. **Intellectual activity is, by definition, intelligent behavior,** although all intelligent behavior is not exclusively intellectual because it may involve other powers besides intellect. Intellectual activity here refers to conception, judgment, and inference. **Conception is the process by which ideas are developed.** Utilizing data from perception, the intellect abstracts the essential from the accidental or superficial characteristics; the conscious expression or formulation of the abstraction gives rise to the idea or concept.[4] A simple example of conception is the idea of triangularity. All triangles have one essential attribute that distinguishes them from circles or squares. When the intellect mentally separates the individual qualities of individual triangles (like size, shape, etc.) from that quality that is essential to all triangles, and when the concept is finally consciously expressed, the thinker understands triangularity—the idea of triangularity is conceptually his.

JUDGMENT

As forms of intellectual activity, judgment and inference are processes to which psychologists and philosophers have not devoted a great deal of time, in spite of the fact that these processes may be considered man's highest intellectual achievements. Fortunately, a detailed understanding of the processes of judgment and inference is not necessary for the exercise of good judgment

[3] *Ibid.,* p. 357.   [4] *Ibid.,* p. 358.

and valid inference. An analogous situation is that of a skilled musician who knows little about the theory of harmony or how or why his musical instrument works, but does an excellent job of rendition anyway.

Let us turn now to judgment. While no attempt can be made here to examine the judgmental process in great detail, some inquiry into its general characteristics should provide a construct for improving one's judgment as well as making him aware of some of the hazards involved in managerial judgment-making.

"Judgment is concerned with the conscious formulation of relationships among sense objects, images, or ideas."[5] What does this mean? In terms of management, we may say that judgment is the process of formulating relationships among facts (existences in the real world) and concepts, or among facts and values (something held in high esteem; a cherished belief; an opinion). Essentially, judgment is a mental process which involves a matching of facts with values. It is a filtering process in which the individual screens the facts he perceives through a system or hierarchy of values which he has built up over his lifetime through experience —the encounters he has had with society. Although the facts one perceives are universal—the fact of A having a watch is also a fact to B—one's interpretation of facts is personal. Why? Because one's values are a way of looking at things; they provide the premises or the criteria by which an individual measures how his judgment fits the facts. This all means that the quality of an individual's judgment is dependent at least upon the following variables: (1) the psychological factors of perception, attitudes, emotion, habits, cultural and social elements, and physical condition; (2) facts; (3) values; (4) the judgmental process terminating in an assertive intellectual act. Thus, poor judgment may result from uncontrolled interferences by these variables. A conscious attempt by the decision-maker to exercise some control over such variables may lead to the improvement of the quality of his judgment. For example, although value judgments cannot be tested objectively, they can be checked for reliability in at least three ways. First, they can be checked against experience. If experience does not seem to support a value judgment or seems

5 *Ibid.*

to give greater support to some other judgment, then one can suspect its reliability. Second, value judgments can be checked against the opinions of the experts—those who have devoted most of their lives to observing and thinking about some phase of human behavior. One who is familiar with some of the best thinking in a field can frequently help the decision-maker to discover blind spots he may be unaware of. Finally, one's system of value judgments can be tested for "internal consistency." If all the value judgments in one's value system are sound, then all of them should be compatible. If two of one's value judgments are incompatible, then both of them cannot be wholly sound.

Knowledge and Judgment

Another way of looking at judgment is to inquire into its relation to knowledge and creativity. Let us first discuss knowledge. Facts alone do not constitute knowledge, because the intellect has not performed the vital function of giving meaning to the facts. Actually, knowledge is a system of values in the sense that an individual constantly weighs new facts against already known facts to determine their meaning. Increasing one's amount of knowledge may increase one's capability for judgment, but its influence upon judgment itself is very probabilistic. For instance, while higher education, which is concerned primarily with the transmission of knowledge, can produce a learned man, it cannot of itself produce a man capable of dealing wisely with his knowledge. A knowledgeable and wise man is a man of decision who understands people's behavior, and who has learned a great deal both through the accumulation of facts and through experience. It is as difficult to learn to make good judgments from a book as it is to learn to make love from a book. Both require trial and error—that is, experience.

Creativity and Judgment

What about creativity and judgment? If the relation between knowledge and judgment is accepted as probabilistic, then the relation between judgment and creativity seems to be more often incompatible than compatible. Why? A high degree of creativity is rarely found in an organization because the traits that make a man creative are frequently resented in a typical organization. The organization man who may have very good judgment may also never have an original idea. Management is as much concerned with the implementation of ideas as it is with the conception of ideas. A manager may be imaginative, having a conceptual skill concerned with the unseen rather than the unborn; and he may be innovative, but he may not have the ability to conceive novel ideas. Moreover, creative persons are less inhibited by the culture and society around them. They express ideas, whereas the organization man is inclined to repress or suppress them. The creative man is more of a nonconformist than a traditionalist. He prefers perceiving to judging, thereby deemphasizing the control and regulation of experience.[6] For the truly creative person, the solution of a problem is not sufficient; it must be elegant.[7]

From the foregoing, it must not be erroneously concluded that all managers are not creative. On the contrary, the somewhat negative comments above emphasize the fact that the truly creative manager is a rarity. He is rare but not nonexistent. If the creative process is one that produces something new, something that has not existed before, with little effort we can recall creative men such as Henry Ford, Andrew Carnegie, Alfred Sloan, Alexander Graham Bell, and Jim Walters. The important point here is that there are few men of such quality.

INFERENCE

The distinction of inference from judgment is not easily specified or generally recognized. Whereas *conception* refers to the intellectual process by which ideas or concepts are developed, and *judgment* is concerned with assertive relationships among facts and values, *inference* constitutes thinking or reasoning. **"It is the process by which new facts are attained from concepts and relationships already apprehended. Inference represents the ex-**

---

[6] T. W. Costello and S. S. Zalkind, *Psychology in Administration* (Englewood Cliffs: Prentice-Hall, 1963), p. 419 from a reprint of "What Makes a Person Creative?" by D. W. MacKinnon in the *Saturday Review*, February 10, 1962, pp. 15-69.

[7] *Ibid.*, p. 421.

tension of knowledge without the mediation of perception."[8] The process of inference takes two well known forms, "induction" and "deduction," which clearly represent the superior intellectual activities of the decision-maker. Yet, few people are conscious of these important processes and their relationships to decision-making. Since a manager is paid to make valid inferences, we should look at the process more closely. We shall first examine premises, because in the process of inference the decision-maker begins with premises.

Premises—The Antecedents of Choice

Premise[9] was first defined by Aristotle. In the Aristotelian sense, a premise is a verbal statement in which something is affirmed or denied; it is an assertion. But not every sentence is a premise. Sentences which express a wish, a question, an exclamation, or a command are not premises because they do not assert an affirmation or a negation. In addition, premises are often confused with the mental acts which they express. This confusion is fostered by using the terms "judgment" and "premise" loosely. A judgment is an intellectual act which is confined to the limits of the mind, and a premise may be regarded as the expression of a judgment. In other words, a premise is the externalization of the judgment which takes place in the mind through expression in words, symbols, signs, and so forth.

A premise which asserts an unqualified agreement or disagreement between two terms—the subject and the predicate—by means of a copula, which is some part of the verb "to be," is called a categorical or unqualified premise. A categorical premise which is the expression of an unqualified judgment consists of three elements: (1) the subject; (2) the predicate; and (3) the copula. The part containing that about which the assertion or denial is made is called the "subject," the part containing that which we affirm or deny is called the "predicate," and the part that relates the subject and the predicate is called the "copula."[10]

---

[8] Harmon, *Principles of Psychology*, p. 359.

[9] The term "premise" will be used in this discussion as found in *The New Century Dictionary:* "Premise . . . an antecedent statement or proposition from which an inference or conclusion is drawn."

[10] These terms as used here have nothing to do with their meaning and use in English grammar. They are used here in the philosophical sense, not

Thus, the "subject" has something said about it; the "predicate" is that which is said about the subject; and the "copula" expresses the act of the intellect in affirming or denying the predicate of the subject at the moment of judgment. For instance, the unqualified statement "the manager is a good human relater" contains a subject (manager), a copula (is), and a predicate (good human relater).

Some premises, however, do not absolutely affirm or deny the predicate of the subject, but do so only conditionally or in case something else is true. This class of conditional premises is composed of a subordinate clause called the antecedent and a principal clause called the consequent—this is the familiar "If . . . then" type of premise. For example, *"If* we lower the price, *then* sales volume will increase." Such a premise is composed of three elements: (1) a cause (the "if" part or antecedent) ; (2) a result or effect (the "then" part or principal clause); and (3), the causal connection which exists between the cause and effect and which is usually only implied in the premise statement.[11]

A decision may also be viewed as a conclusion reached from factual and/or value premises. This classification of premises is based upon the nature of their content rather than upon the nature of the assertion as is the case with categorical and conditional premises. **A factual premise is one that is predominantly measured by objective standards, whereas a value premise is measured by personal or nonempirical standards.** This means that a premise may be almost wholly factual or almost wholly value, or partly factual and partly value. A premise or a part of a premise which is measured by objective standards is one that can, in theory, be tested by some means other than one's personal standards, such as a generally agreed upon common denominator or criterion. For instance, if an executive making a proposal suggested that a company would lose $10,000, each administrator present would visualize essentially the same thing—namely, that $10,000 of the company's resources would disappear if that alternative were to be pursued. The dollar as a measure is ex-

---

in the grammatical sense. See Morris R. Cohen and Ernest Nagel, *An Introduction to Logic and Scientific Method* (New York: Harcourt, 1934) , p. 30.

[11] M. H. Jones, *Executive Decision-Making* (Homewood: Irwin, 1961) , pp. 57-59.

ternal and explicit, and it is accepted in the United States as the unit of monetary value. It is objective and nobody questions it. Yet the relative value of $10,000 to each executive would vary.

A value premise or part of a value premise, on the other hand, is one that is measured by one's own private measuring system. All of us have gradually accumulated subjective measures based upon our varying backgrounds and experiences. As a result, each person has a different conceptual structure by which he makes his value judgments. Thus, we frequently hear the statement, "He made a value judgment" when someone does not agree with somebody's else's opinion. Actually, in decision-making there is no escape from making value judgments because virtually every premise contains some degree of value characteristics. Moreover, even if we assume that we are dealing with purely factual premises in decision-making, it is continually necessary to choose premises whose truth or falsity cannot be determined with certainty with the data and time available for reaching the decision. The most serious difficulty with value measures, however, is that most of us think of our own value standards as factual or objective; we frequently assume that everyone else uses the same value scale or value structure as we do. Nothing could be further from the truth.

Induction and Deduction

Although most men mingle inductive and deductive methods in thought processes, the two terms are clearly distinguishable, and are the major forms of inference. As the word "induction" indicates, to think or reason inductively is to be led from one position to another until a decision is reached. **Induction, then, is the process of inference in which the decision-maker reasons from individual instances to a generalization or general conclusion.** He observes a series of phenomena until a pattern begins to emerge and a provisional generalization may be formed. It is the process underlying all attempts to solve problems empirically, that is, by experience and by experiment.

Unlike induction which proceeds from individual instances to a generalization, **deduction is reasoning from the general to the particular or, more specifically, from stated premises to a conclusion.** These stated premises may be general truths, general laws, principles, or already existing generalizations. Although the processes of induction and deduction seem to go in opposite directions, an intimate relation exists between them. Reasoning about problems combines building up generalizations from instances or data (induction) and applying generalizations to instances (deduction) in a kaleidoscopic mixture. In this connection Morris Cohen and Ernest Nagel state:

> . . . deduction is not concerned with the truth or falsity of its premises, while the characteristic nature of induction is to be concerned with just that. Induction may therefore be viewed as the method by means of which the material truth of the premises is established.[12]

Induction thus furnishes the factual materials and generalizations which may then serve as premises for deduction. Generalizations reached in one series of observations or experiments may be used deductively to formulate a further generalization in the form of a hypothesis or alternative. Then inductive procedures such as examining particular instances may be used to collect evidence relevant to that alternative. Following appropriate analysis of the data, a generalization may be reached which either supports or rejects the originating hypothesis or alternative. But even this explanation is too simple, because deduction may be introduced at any point. As a matter of fact, deduction may be introduced any time during the inductive stage because principles, laws, or already existing generalizations may be used in collecting the data, in the acceptance or rejection of data, and in the analysis and evaluation of facts.

Induction and Decision-Making

As indicated above, facts are the raw materials of induction. Actually, an abundance or sufficiency of relevant factual materials is usually necessary to support a generalization. In addition to the mere perception of facts, facts must also be analyzed and interpreted, classified and described, and summarized. Through these processes the decision-maker may gain considerable insight into the material nature or truth of his data and may thus be in a position to make a useful generalization from the facts. Such

---

[12] Cohen and Nagel, *An Introduction to Logic and Scientific Method*, p. 278.

generalizations are inductions which he has abstracted from his data and which he supposes to be valid and true. This "inductive ascent" in which the decision-maker proceeds from his mass of facts to generalizations is a psychological process; that is, the facts do not generalize themselves—the manager generalizes from the instances or facts. Let us explore this further.

When a generalization is inferred from a limited number of instances, the process obviously can be only probable, not certain. However, the probability of the inference may be increased by additional evidence as the enumeration of instances approaches completeness. The statistical method, which is a method of dealing with instances or observations, is an example of a quantitative method which can lead to inductive statistical inferences. When statistics on employment, unemployment, labor turnover, industrial accidents, investment yields, working capital, inventory, cancer, accidental automobile deaths, or any other phenomena are cited, instances are being used. One unemployed person is one instance. One-half million unemployed reported in a given area are one-half million instances. Sometimes we take particular instances in some group and enumerate them completely. We then infer a general statement regarding the whole class or genus to which they belong. For example, we observe that steel, copper, aluminum, and silver conduct heat. We conclude, therefore, that all metal conducts heat. It now makes sense to us why cooking utensils are made of metal, why the exteriors of homes are usually brick or wood (not metal), and why metal chairs are hot and uncomfortable to sit in during the summer months. While inferences may be made from a single instance, or from a sample, or from millions of instances, or from all the instances in a group or class, in general rational induction relies upon a multiplicity of instances to support the generalization. This need for a multiplicity of facts indicates that a *search for order among the facts* in a problematic situation to facilitate the "inductive ascent" is necessary. In this connection, Cohen and Nagel assert that:

. . . an analysis of the situation (problematic) must be made into a certain number of factors, present or absent, which are believed to be relevant to the solution of the problem. Now the order among the facts for which we are in search is expressible . . . in the form: C (cause) is invariably connected with E (effect). And this means that no factor can be regarded as a cause if it is present while the effect is absent, or if it is absent while the effect is present, or if it varies in some manner while the effect does not vary in some corresponding manner.[13]

John Stuart Mill gave a more explicit expression to this "invariable connection" between cause and effect in his "experimental methods." He summarized his teaching in five "canons" of induction:

The Method of Agreement: If two or more instances of the phenomenon under investigation have only one circumstance in common, the circumstance in which alone all the instances agree, is the cause (or effect) of the given phenomenon. *The Method of Difference:* If an instance in which the phenomenon under investigation occurs, and an instance in which it does not occur, have every circumstance in common save one, that one occurring only in the former: the circumstance in which alone the two instances differ is the effect, or cause, or an indispensable part of the cause, of the phenomenon. *The Joint Method of Agreement and Difference:* If two or more instances in which the phenomenon occurs have only one circumstance in common, while two or more instances in which it does not occur have nothing in common save the absence of that circumstance: the circumstance in which alone the two sets of instances differ is the effect, or cause, or an indispensable part of the cause, of the phenomenon. *The Method of Concomitant Variation:* Whatever phenomenon varies in any manner whenever another phenomenon varies in some particular manner, is either a cause or an effect of that phenomenon, or is connected with it through some fact of causation. *The Method of Residues:* Subduct from any phenomenon such part as is known by previous inductions to be the effect of certain antecedents, and the residue of the phenomenon is the effect of the remaining antecedents.[14]

Although these canons are distillations of common sense, Mill claimed too much for them. Mill not only believed that the use of his canons could discover the order in which facts stand to one another, but he also maintained that all inferences are made by means of these canons. Moreover, he believed that his methods had a demonstrative or proof function; it was claimed that an induction was valid and absolutely certain if it conformed to the

[13] *Ibid.*, p. 250

[14] John Stuart Mill, *A System of Logic* (London: Harrison, 1843), II, Chapter VIII.

"experimental methods." For such high claims Mill has been severely criticized by many philosophers. For example, the fault of the Method of Agreement is the fact that a phenomenon may have several causes. The Method of Difference cannot guarantee with certainty that the sufficient conditions for a phenomenon have been found because the factor noted may be only a "necessary part" of the cause. The Joint Method of Agreement and Difference simply combines the limitations of the first two methods. The Method of Concomitant Variation can be employed only if degrees or magnitudes of effects and causes can be distinguished. Finally, since the Method of Residues derives its conclusions from inductions (premises) already established, this method actually operates as a deductive process. Yet, while Mill's methods do have the defects that I have pointed out, they are nevertheless of considerable value in eliminating irrelevant facts in the process of searching for order and relevance among the facts.

Deduction and Decision-Making

Deduction as a form of inference represents the process that employs a form called the "syllogism." It is the heart of the deductive process and is a group of three assertions, of which one follows from the other two if certain conditions are met in the formulation of these premises and their relation to each other. Deduction, and consequently the syllogism, are not concerned with the material truth or falsity of the premises (this is the role of induction) with which it deals, but rather with the *validity* of the decisions made from these premises. It can be said of a valid syllogism that if the premises are true, then the decision also is true and valid. If the premises are false, then the decision is valid (from a logical point of view) but false since truth does not spring from falsity. Thus, deduction does not concern itself in any way with the truth of the premises, but only about the *cogency* of the argument. This shows that the conclusion follows as a necessary consequence of the relationship which exists among the premises. Indeed, the conclusion is no more than the expression of that relationship. Consequently, the "form" of the syllogism is the nexus between the two premises and the conclusion; it is the sequence, the conclusive force, the convincing power, that binds the conclusion to the premises. It follows, then, that if the reasoning mind admits the premises, it must likewise admit the conclusion.

The foregoing discussion shows the importance of having some awareness of the deductive process.[15] If the decision-maker understands something of the theory of the syllogism as an abbreviated mode of deduction, he will undoubtedly know when he deviates from its theory as well as when he does not. Consequently, he should not expect his decisions to be any better than the process he used to arrived at them. If he uses no deduction, then of course he cannot be sure of a valid reasoning process, and his decisions could be both untrue and invalid. Indeed, invalid decisions from a reasoning point of view possess a quality not possessed by valid decisions—there is no possibility that invalid decisions are true, unless they are true independently of the premises because of luck or chance. This means that the apparent premises and decisions are not related to one another at all. On the other hand, a valid decision resulting from a valid reasoning process has at least a possibility of being true because of the veracity of the deductive process. It therefore follows that very careful attention must be directed to the formation of true premises if decisions are to be true as well as logically valid. So rests the case for deduction—a process that functions like a set of spotlights probing the insecure fastenings of every managerial and personal decision.

Appendix. Some Notes on Deductive Method

1. A syllogism contains three assertions: a major premise, a minor premise, and a conclusion.
2. There are two kinds of syllogisms: the categorical (unqualified) and the hypothetical (qualified).
3. The categorical syllogism contains three terms: the major term, the minor term, and the middle term. To be valid, the

---

[15] Without discussing the technical details which may be found in any elementary logic textbook such as R. J. Kreyche, *Logic,* rev. ed. (New York: Holt, 1961), a number of additional points on the deductive method may be found in the appendix to this chapter.

terms of a categorical syllogism must be arranged according to certain rules. **Reasoning in this case is essentially a process of comparison in which the minor and major terms are compared with the middle term.** Good reasoning here is actually the search for good middle terms. For example, if $B = C$ and $A = B$, then $A = C$. In this case $B = C$ is the major premise with C as the major term; $A = B$ is the minor premise with A as the minor term; the middle term B appears in both the major and minor premises but not in the conclusion $A = C$. The subsequent recognition and pronouncement of a new relationship in the comparison of the major and minor terms with the middle term is a "mediated judgment," constituting the decision. This act is a judgment because it is an assertion of the relationship discovered between the minor and major terms; and it is a *mediated judgment* because this relationship is not discovered directly by an immediate comparison of the minor and major terms, but by a comparison of them with the common middle term.

4. The most important kind of hypothetical syllogism for our purposes is the conditional one. The major premise is of the "if A (antecedent), then B (consequent)" type mentioned earlier in this chapter. The minor premise and the conclusion are categorical statements. The validity of this type of reasoning process is dependent upon the relation existing between the antecedent and the consequent in the major premise. In a conditional syllogism the minor premise must either affirm the antecedent or deny the consequent. That is, if the minor premise affirms the antecedent of the conditional major premise, then the conclusion must affirm the consequent; and, if the minor premise denies the consequent of the conditional major premise, the conclusion must deny the antecedent.

5. Syllogistic rules must be followed in deduction. Categorical syllogisms have general rules, while hypothetical syllogisms have their own special rules. Logic textbooks include many proofs for these rules.

6. A state of *logical implication* must exist for one to emerge from the deductive process with a "validating form" of syllogism. This means that the arrangement of the premises and

the terms of the premises are according to certain logical properties (called "figures" and "moods" of the syllogism) so that the truth or falsity of one or more premises limits the truth or falsity of other premises. Thus, the assertion that a decision is valid if it is based upon an implication means that the arrangement of the premises and its terms is such as to warrant the validity or falsity of the decision.

7. Deductive inferences or conclusions are not necessarily truthful. If the premises are true and the reasoning valid, then the conclusion will be valid and true. If the premises are false and the reasoning valid, then the conclusion is valid from a reasoning point of view but false from an empirical point of view. If the premises are false and the reasoning invalid, then the conclusion is both invalid and false. If the premises are true and the reasoning invalid, then the conclusion is invalid from a logical point of view, but may be true independently of the reasoning process; that is, for reasons external to the deductive process. Thus, invalid reasoning does not necessarily lead to false conclusions. Also, the decision-maker must search for true premises if he wishes not only valid inferences but also true conclusions. The decision-maker cannot get more out of his premises than is contained therein.

8. A limitation related to the truth of the premises is worth mentioning. Complete logical systems may be developed, reasoned validly, and generally accepted in a given culture, and yet depend entirely upon a given set of values. For instance, an entire economic system may be developed from a given set of premises and accepted by most people within the society. But there are other economic systems developed from other premises and accepted by most people within other societies. Both systems may be quite satisfactory from the objective view of the production manager in each culture. Yet depending upon how one measures values, one system may seem to give greater output, productivity, and perhaps even a higher standard of living.

9. Making use of the relevant contributions of deduction is, nevertheless, one way of minimizing arbitrary opinion. It is a good idea to clarify our concepts by asking for the precise meaning of our words, and to try to check our "favorite

ideas" by applying them to accurately formulated premises. To a really good manager of above average intelligence, syllogistic deductions may be so obvious and take place so quickly that he may scarcely be aware of their existence. But not everybody is extremely intelligent. Hence for most administrators making correct deductions is a problem.

10. No sensible person who has the techniques of logical manipulation at his command would knowingly tackle a difficult problem without using them. Logic's test of "internal consistency" (there can be no leakage of truth in a valid deductive process) and its convenience for handling deductive inferences are indisputable. Of course, we cannot say that managers trained in this inferential process will not make mistakes. But it is encouraging to note that sound logic will help insure valid steps in carrying out the deductive process. The big mistakes are made in the formulation of premises. Deduction, unfortunately, is no protection against the misinterpretation of empirical reality. One of the advantages of the logical medium is that we are forced to examine our premises. Yet none of the precautions of logical methodology can prevent organizational life or personal life from being an adventure. However, the deductive process does enable many people to be more certain in their decisions.

11. The syllogism, which is the chief contribution of the deductive method, serves the decision-maker in two important capacities. First, it performs the indispensable function of a means of testing an alternative. As such, the syllogism may be considered a generalized formula for logical requirements that must be satisfied if an alternative is stated in premise form and is to be accepted as valid. In other words, the syllogistic form is useful because it serves as a check in decision-making, holding up the logical conditions to be satisfied. Second, it may be used to suggest experimental combinations of premises. That is, the decision-maker may take a premise and combine it with others to see where the reasoning will lead him (the conclusion in one syllogism may become a premise in another syllogism, and so on). The process need not be strictly valid (for example, when a categorical syllogism has an undistributed middle term, that is, the middle

term is not once taken in its full meaning in the syllogism) because the decision is usually only probabilistic anyway. It is a serious misunderstanding of the syllogism to make it a dictator in decision-making, where probable decisions have great practical significance.

Discussion Questions

1. Distinguish between "intellect" and "intelligence." What is meant by "intellectual activity"?
2. Distinguish among "conception," "judgment," and "inference."
3. How are "knowledge" and "creativity" related to judgment?
4. What is a premise? Why are premises called "antecedents of choice"?
5. Distinguish between a premise and a judgment.
6. Name the types of premises mentioned in the chapter. Explain each type.
7. What are some of the problems people get into with respect to values?
8. What is induction? What is deduction? Elaborate on the distinction between the two.
9. What is meant by the "inductive ascent"?
10. What is a syllogism? What is it made up of? List the types of syllogisms. Briefly discuss each.
11. If B = C and A = B, why does A = C?
12. What is meant by "logical implication"?
13. Is deduction of any value in the real world of managerial decision-making? If so, how?
14. Are deductive inferences necessarily truthful? Explain your answer.
15. Can managers be logical without exposure to logic and scientific method? Explain.
16. Of what use are "Mill's methods"?
17. Why have psychologists not devoted a great deal of time to the thought processes?
18. "Psychologists are concerned with how we *actually* think; logicians with how we *should* think." Discuss.

19. "Deduction is no protection against the misinterpretation of reality." Explain.
20. "The decision-maker cannot get more out of his premises than is contained therein." Explain.

References

Ambrose, A., and M. Laserowitz, *Fundamentals of Symbolic Logic*. (New York: Rinehart, 1948).

Bachhuber, Andrew, *Introduction to Logic* (New York: Appleton, 1957).

Brown, Ray E., *Judgment in Administration* (New York: McGraw-Hill, 1966), Chapter 1.

Carnap, Rudolf, *The Nature and Application of Inductive Logic* (Chicago: University of Chicago Press, 1950).

Cohen, Morris R., and Ernest Nagel, *An Introduction to Logic and Scientific Method* (New York: Harcourt, 1934).

Costello, T. W., and S. S. Zalkind, *Psychology in Administration* (Englewood Cliffs: Prentice-Hall, 1963), Parts 1, 2, 3, 5, 6.

Davis, Ralph Currier, *The Fundamentals of Top Management* (New York: Harper, 1951).

Dewey, John, *Logic: The Theory of Inquiry* (New York: Holt, 1938).

Harmon, Francis L., *Principles of Psychology*, rev. ed. (Milwaukee: Bruce, 1951), Chapters 6, 7, 12.

Jones, Manley H., *Executive Decision-Making* (Homewood: Irwin, 1961), Chapter 2.

Kreyche, Robert J., *Logic*, rev. ed. (New York: Holt, 1961).

Maritain, Jacques, *Formal Logic* (New York: Sheed and Ward, 1946).

Maziarz, Edward A., *The Philosophy of Mathematics* (New York: Philosophical Library, 1950).

Mill, John Stuart, *A System of Logic* (London: Harrison, 1843), II, Chapter VIII).

Smith, Vincent E., *The Elements of Logic* (Milwaukee: Bruce, 1956).

Toohey, J. H., "Propositions, Judgment, and Inference," *The*

Journal of Philosophy, XXXVII, No. 9 (April, 1940), pp. 232-243.

Turner, William, *Lessons in Logic* (Washington, D.C.: Catholic Education Press, 1911).

Vinacke, W. E., *The Psychology of Thinking* (New York: Mc-Graw-Hill, 1952), Chapters 6, 9.

Chapter 8. **The Pattern of Decision**

..

Chapter 8

The Pattern of Decision

Human nature cannot know the mystery of an art
without experience.—PLATO

··

Looking up from the bottom of the managerial hierarchy, it may
appear that decisions of managers and administrators are the arbitrary products of impulse and caprice. This should not be the
case. A managerial decision should be based upon premises.
Sometimes these premises may not be precisely formulated, or
may not even be operative at the conscious level. But as I have
already stated, a correct and compelling decision is not a simple,
unsupported assertion; rather, it is a decision sustained by the
premises from which it is derived.

But the activity of decision-making does not begin with the
formulation of premises. Earlier stages involve such considerations as uncertainty and doubt, factual analysis, consciousness of
a problem, definition of the problem, and so forth. It is important
here that we begin our study with the factors which initiate
decision-making. For, as F. S. C. Northrop so aptly points out:

One may have the most rigorous of methods during the later stages of
investigation but if a false or superficial beginning has been made,
rigor later on will never retrieve the situation.[1]

To begin, let us consider the point at which we are aware of
uncertainty or doubt.

UNCERTAINTY

Uncertainty or doubt is the first stage in the decision-making
process. It is likely to be an anxious one, a period of worry,

[1] F. S. C. Northrop, *The Logic of the Sciences and the Humanities* (New
York: Macmillan, 1947), p. 1.

anxiety, and confusion. We are doubtful because the situation facing us is uncertain and doubtful. This kind of uncertainty is not the subjective or negative personal state of self-made doubt, as is depression, for example. On the contrary, this concept of uncertainty is a positive one, stemming from a doubtful situation which is objective and external to us. But where does the uncertainty come from? It comes from a situation, the elements of which are neither settled nor coherent, and which lacks unity that is capable of bringing the process of decision-making into existence.[2]

An uncertain situation occurs when we find ourselves somewhat overwhelmed by a mass of seemingly contradictory facts that appear to need explanation and unification, or when we face a situation that is unpleasant or frustrating, which we feel we must do something about but which we seem to approach with a numb sterility of mind. For example, a failure to achieve some organizational goal, as evidenced by declining profits, may impose itself upon us with a formidable array of facts—revenue facts, cost and expense facts, product facts, market facts, competition facts, organization facts, and so on. We become confused, worried, and vague; our minds go blank (a normal but frustrating experience during the stage of uncertainty) as we feel completely inadequate to cope with the situation at this moment. If the manager decides for any number of reasons such as time, cost, or effort that nothing should now be done about the perplexing situation, then of course the decision-making pattern is cut short and abandoned. On the other hand, if the individual feels that the uncertain situation is one which needs to be settled or resolved, then he must push on into the next stage of decision-making. The beginning of the transition from an uncertain situation to a resolved situation occurs in the stage of analysis and definition.

ANALYSIS AND DEFINITION

When the manager judges that an uncertain situation is a *problematic* situation for him, he has decided through his own

[2] John Dewey, *Logic: The Theory of Inquiry* (New York: Holt, 1938), pp. 105-107.

judgment that the situation generates a problem or difficulty
which is worthy of his attention and study. This is a very important point, because the judgment which qualifies an uncertain
situation as problematic for the decision-maker not only is an
acknowledgment of the existence of a problem but is also the
first step toward its solution. Therefore, judging an uncertain
situation as problematic means that what was originally doubtful
is now already partially settled, because the process of establish-
ing a problem has been initiated.

After acknowledging the existence of a problem, the decision-
maker must analyze the problematic situation. Such an analysis
should guide the investigator to the facts necessary to understand
the problem clearly and precisely. It is through the careful analysis of the problematic situation that the manager is led to what
may be called the **relevant factual situation—the situation which
contains the relevant facts to which his analysis and study has
led him.**

With the uncertain situation qualified by judgment as problematic, and with the problematic situation reduced to the relevant factual situation by analysis, the administrator is now ready
to *describe* the relevant facts. Observed facts are undescribed.
facts; they are perceived by observation but are not yet put into
verbal or symbolic form. The moment merely "observed facts"
are abstracted and expressed in words or symbols they become
"described facts." Facts are described so that they may be communicated and may take the form of premises and, consequently,
provide the type of material to which the methods of logic and
mathematics can be applied.

The analytical process in this stage is largely a factual analysis,
in which the individual's first task is to separate the relevant,
the material, and the significant from the irrelevant, immaterial,
and trivial. Here the manager must discriminate between fact
and assumption or opinion. In this respect, it should be noted
again that although facts are universal, interpretations of facts
are personal. The decision-maker should be aware that his analysis of facts is dominated to a great extent by his conceptual
framework—his own system of ideas. The concepts and values he
brings to the facts determine for him what facts are relevant and
significant and what facts are not. At this point he must be

careful of manufacturing facts (discussed in Chapter 4 under management by the scientific method). Again, this occurs when the decision-maker has prejudged a situation, and wishes to build a case for his prejudgment or volitional choice by providing an illusory factual base that appears to support the prejudgment. This is what psychologists call "rationalization."

The analysis of facts takes place in a few moments or over a period of years, depending upon the problematic situation being analyzed and the breadth and complexity of the problem. Yet the factual analysis is only the first task of this stage. The next task, equally difficult, is the definition or specification of the problem. The outcome of the factual analysis of the situation generating the problem should be a precise definition of the problem— stating it in the form of a question to make it definite and specific. If the decision-maker is unable to state the problem specifically, preferably in one interrogative sentence which includes one or more goals to be achieved, such as, "How can the efficiency of Department B be improved so as to decrease costs?" then the analysis of the problematic situation has not been adequate or of sufficient depth. In this case, further analysis is necessary.

Throughout this entire stage the decision-maker must constantly be on guard against the following: emotional excitement, bias, habits, and the tendency of human beings to seek the road of least resistance. These and other human frailties may result in a superficial analysis followed by a statement of the *apparent problem* (what appears to be the problem) rather than the *real problem* (the actual problem). Many an excellent solution to an apparent problem will not work in practice because it is the solution to a problem which does not exist in the real world. Actually, a short-circuiting of the factual analysis may result in a person's having to spend more time in the future to solve the real problem when he returns for further analysis. The survival or continued success of any organization depends upon the ability of its managers to discover real problems as they are projected in a complex and dynamic environment (discussed in Chapter 3). A real problem well stated in one interrogative sentence is already partially solved, for it directs a person to the area where a solution should be sought. For instance, to solve a short-term working capital problem created by inadequate cash flow, one would not ordinarily seek a solution in the area of physical manufacturing processes. Or, to solve a morale problem caused by a man's attitude, one would not look in the research and product-development area.

CREATING ALTERNATIVES

With his previous knowledge, plus a sufficiency of relevant facts, and with the problem defined and delimited, the decider is now ready to atempt to create tentative solutions or relevant alternatives. While we may have ideas at any time or stage of the decision-making process, relevant suggestions for solutions are stimulated by the awareness of definite and relevants facts, a well organized conceptual framework, a specific problem, and the indeterminate uncertainties of the situation.

As far as ideas or alternatives are concerned, it is interesting to note that our ideas differ according to the level of reflection reached. At first our ideas are vague, one might even say "half-baked," but with further observation and reflection they become more suitable as a means of solving the problem (s) . As ideas become more appropriate, our perceptions also become more acute. Perception and conception thus work together until perception locates, describes, and circumscribes the problem, while conception, judgment, and inference together form the means for the creation of relevant alternative solutions.

The next step is to estimate and develop the consequences of the alternatives. Can the entertained alternatives be the means of solving the problem? A verbal or symbolic expression of the alternatives helps to determine whether a given alternative can function as a solution. Additional factual material might be needed at this point. A critical examination of the consequences of alternatives may result in the rejection, acceptance, or modification of ideas in an attempt to arrive at more relevant alternatives. Here the manager attempts to appraise the pertinency of the facts and the alternatives. Facts are tested by their relevance as evidence. Ideas are tested by their capacity to bring new facts to light, to organize selected facts into coherent wholes, and to function as possible solutions to problems.[3]

[3] *Ibid.*, pp. 113-114.

Creating and figuring out alternatives and their consequences is a major part of all decision-making. Nevertheless, in spite of the primary importance of the use of alternatives in deciding, no definitive rule can be laid down for hitting upon relevant alternatives. We do not know yet how the mind organizes, relates, and synthesizes facts and ideas. However, we do know that after a period of prolonged conscious study and analysis, a period of incubation sets in. Often this is when the decision-maker ceases his deliberate effort to solve the problem and turns his attention to other activities such as recreation, sleep, physical exercise, or other mental work. Time is essential to the process as the manager mulls over facts and experimentally modifies, casts, and recasts his ideas. The length of time depends upon the competence of the thinker, the nature of the problem, and the complexity of the initiating situation.

While there are no definite or sure-fire rules for coming up with relevant ideas, there are nevertheless several ways to enhance the probability of creating alternatives. First, the decision-maker should realize that alternatives are a function, at least in part, of the facts and concepts at his disposal. Accordingly, he should collect as much background information about the problem as he can. When he has sufficient data and ideas, fruitful alternatives may emerge. Second, he should concentrate on the problem intensively for prolonged periods, preferably eagerly and without anxiety; then he should turn away from the problem and relax. Tension and anxiety have a negative effect on one's creative ability, while relaxation has a positive effect. It might be a good idea for the individual to carry a notebook or a $3'' \times 5''$ card so that he can record the core of a good idea at any time such as on the fairway or tennis court. Failure to do this often results in the loss of many of our best ideas because we depend upon one of the frailest of the human faculties—the memory. Third, if the decider feels he has reached a complete impasse, it may be helpful to restructure the problem. Restructuring involves rearranging the elements of a problem, including a revision of the problem statement, a change in viewpoint, such as looking at the problem as the other fellow sees it, or a permissible modification of objectives (s). Such activities may stimulate alternatives not previously thought of. Moreover, since alternatives are partly a function of one's total background, the decision-maker should take advantage of every opportunity to build up his conceptual structure through education, experience, reading, and discussion. A well organized conceptual system is his sword for the battle of choice; we should try to keep it sharp. Also, the creating of alternatives will be more productive for the individual who courageously and frequently attempts to solve increasingly more and more difficult problems in the future.

VERIFICATION

The fourth stage of decision-making is verification. In this stage, the manager attempts to reexamine, confirm, substantiate, verify, and test the alternatives created and developed in the preceding stage. This stage of verification rests on the principle that a period of hesitation before the adoption of any alternative in order to check the alternatives for soundness is a characteristic of the rational approach to deciding. Most of us have had the disillusioning experience of realizing that an alternative or idea which looked good initially was quite impracticable upon verification.

Verification of alternatives may be accomplished informally by the imaginative projection of the possible desirable and undesirable effects if an alternative were actually put into action. A more formalized system of verification is the method of deduction discussed in Chapter 7. Deduction serves admirably as such a check, setting up the logical conditions or standards that must be satisfied if an alternative is to be accepted as the best choice. To achieve this more formalized verification, alternatives should be verbally or symbolically stated in premise form in order to discover the implications of the alternatives and to permit the drawing of valid inferences from them.

IMPLEMENTATION

Nothing is more useless than good decisions that disappear into file cabinets or that are quietly sabotaged by those who should execute them. Unfortunately, many decision-makers seem anxious to get on to the next problem and leave the important work of implementation to others. In this connection, it should be kept in mind that a good decision badly implemented may be worse than a bad decision expertly implemented.[4] This fifth stage of decision-making can make or break an otherwise useful decision; it should therefore be as carefully planned and controlled as possible.

The decision-maker may find that the familiar technique of "role-playing" is useful in implementing a decision. He may secure someone to play the role of interviewee while he attempts to anticipate the possible responses of a subordinate to his communications about the execution of the decision. The decision-maker can sit back and reflect on the upcoming interview and attempt to anticipate the reactions of the interviewee. In addition, the decision-maker should make every effort to maximize the chances of occurrence of all of the favorable consequences which he thought of in the preceding stage. Finally, he should seek to minimize the effects of all of the disadvantages which he predicted for the decision.

SUMMARY

The pattern of decision-making thus includes the following five stages:

1. Uncertainty
2. Analysis and definition
3. Creating alternatives
4. Verification
5. Implementation

Stage 1—the stage of uncertainty—is a function of the state of development of a decision-maker's conceptual structure. A person who has a well developed conceptual framework is sensitive to doubtful and uncertain situations, while one who has a badly constructed system of ideas may not be fully aware of an unsettled situation and its accompanying problem. In stage 2—the stage of analysis and definition—the decision-maker seeks to discover the

---

[4] K. E. Schnelle, *Case Analysis and Business Problem Solving* (New York: McGraw-Hill, 1967) , pp. 98-99.

relevant facts of the problematic situation, and to define and delimit the problem. The statement of the problem in this stage, plus a sufficiency of relevant facts and the decision-maker's previous knowledge, may then act as stimuli for the creation of relevant alternatives—stage 3. In stage 4—the stage of verification —the decision-maker attempts some form of testing the alternatives proposed in stage 3. Whether he chooses to check his alternatives formally or informally is up to him, but he must use some method of checking at this point. Finally, the decision-maker must concern himself with the important aspect of implementation or execution of the decision. The decision-maker's role here is much like that of an architect—a role of active supervision. He needs to prepare himself and others for changes that may be needed in the effective communication and execution of the decision.

Although the preceding pattern of decision-making appears in five neat stages, the reader should realize that in actual practice these five stages often overlap. For example, it is not uncommon for an alternative or idea to occur while the administrator is still collecting data about the problem. In complex problems, different phases of the subject may develop at different rates. For example, the decider may have reached the verification stage for one aspect of a major problem, while he is still in the stage of analysis and definition on another aspect or subsidiary part of the major problem. Nevertheless, it is necessary to approach the pattern of decision-making stage by stage to analyze the process and to develop insights into the solution of a problem.

Discussion Questions

1. What is meant by a pattern of decision-making?
2. What are the stages of decision-making? Is this the only pattern of decision-making? Explain.
3. Distinguish between an uncertain situation and a problematic situation.
4. Distinguish between observed facts and described facts.
5. What is an apparent problem? What is a real problem?

6. Discuss stages 1, 2, and 3 of the decision-making process.
7. What are some hints for coming up with relevant alternatives?
8. What role does tension play in creating alternatives?
9. What role does relaxation play in creating alternatives?
10. What is meant by verification? What is meant by implementation?
11. Why is the "beginning" so important in decision-making?
12. What is the "relevant factual situation?"
13. What is a problem?
14. Why should a problem be defined?
15. "At first, our ideas are vague." Explain.
16. What practices may one employ to enhance the probability of coming up with relevant alternatives?
17. What is meant when we say that our ideas become "refined" after some reflection?
18. What is meant by restructuring the problem?
19. Of what use is "role-playing" in implementation of decisions?
20. "In actual practice, the stages of decision-making may overlap." Discuss.

References

Cohen, Morris R., and Ernest Nagel, *An Introduction to Logic and Scientific Method* (New York: Harcourt, 1934) .

Dewey, John, *Logic: The Theory of Inquiry* (New York: Holt, 1938, Part 2) .

Dewey, John, "Inquiry and Indeterminateness of Situations," *The Journal of Philosophy*, XXXIX, No. 11 (May, 1942) , 290-296.

Drucker, Peter, "How to Make a Business Decision," *Nation's Business*, Vol. 44, No. 4 (April, 1956) , 38, 39, 68-71.

Durkin, Helen, "Trial and Error, Gradual Analysis and Sudden Reorganization," *Archives of Psychology*, XXX, No. 210 (May, 1937) , 5-38.

Hurni, M. L., "Decision-Making in the Age of Automation," *Harvard Business Review*, XXXIII, No. 5 (September, 1955), 49-58.

Hutchins, Robert M., "The Task of the Administrator is Ordering the Means to an End," *Modern Hospital,* No. 71 (November, 1948), 51-54.

Johnson, Donald M., "A Modern Account of Problem-Solving," *The Psychological Bulletin,* XLI, No. 4 (April, 1944), 201-299.

Katona, G., "Psychological Analysis of Business Decisions and Expectations," *The American Economic Review,* XXXVI, No. 1 (March, 1946), 44-62.

Lefford, Arthur, "The Influence of Emotional Subject Matter on Logical Reasoning," *Journal of General Psychology,* XXXIV, Second Half (April, 1946), 127-151.

Morell, R. W., *Managerial Decision-Making* (Milwaukee: Bruce, 1960), Chapters 3-9.

Morell, R. W., "Analysis of Stages in Decision-Making," *Research Bulletin No. 106,* University of Detroit Press (January, 1958), 1-12.

Morgan, John J., and James T. Morton, "The Distortion of Syllogistic Reasoning Produced by Personal Convictions," *The Journal of Social Psychology,* XX, First Half (August, 1944), 39-59.

Northrop, F. S. C., *The Logic of the Sciences and The Humanities* (New York: Macmillan, 1947).

Oppenheim, Felix E., "Rational Choice," *Journal of Philosophy,* Vol. 50, No. 12 (1953), 341-350.

Schnelle, K. E., *Case Analysis and Business Problem Solving* (New York: McGraw-Hill, 1967), Chapters 2, 3, 4, 5.

Simon, Herbert A., *Administrative Behavior,* 2nd ed. (New York: Macmillan, 1955), Chapters 3-5.

Tannenbaum, Robert, "Managerial Decision-Making," *The Journal of Business,* XXIII, No. 1 (January, 1950), 22-39.

Chapter 9. A Model for Management

Outline of a Model for Decision-Making
- I. Statements of Relevant Facts
- II. The Statement of the Problem
- III. Statements of Alternatives
- IV. Final Decision
- V. Final Verification
- VI. Implementation

The Model and Implementing Procedures

The Model in Application

Appendices (A, B, C)

Discussion Questions

References

Chapter 9

A Model for Management

"Wit is the salt of conversation,
not the food."—WILLIAM HAZLITT

The description and analysis of the pattern of decision-making in
Chapter 8 was made to provide a basis for the development of a
model for managerial decision-making. My idea was to present
the pattern of decision at length for expository reasons and then
present the model, for I feel that this is the approach that will
make the model most meaningful to the reader. Let us now use
the pattern to develop a model in outline form. Of course, everyone will not agree with the model as to its format, as to its steps,
or as to the sequence of its steps. Nevertheless, I am aware of this
and present the following model as representing only one
approach.

OUTLINE OF A MODEL FOR DECISION-MAKING

I. Statements of relevant facts. These should be terse yet complete. Enumerate the statements: 1, 2, . . . ; keep them to a
single line, or at most two lines, if at all possible.

II. The statement of the problem. Preferably, this should be a
single interrogative sentence, and should specify one or more
goals.

III. Statements of alternatives available (with advantages and
disadvantages) :
1. The —— Company should . . .
   1.1. *Advantages:* (enumerate; try to state each in one or
   two lines)
   1.2. *Disadvantages:* (enumerate, as Advantages)

173

2. The —— Company should . . . (enumerate further alternatives if they exist, with Advantages and Disadvantages)

IV. Final decision, preferably a one-sentence statement of the alternative selected.

V. Final verification, a brief statement of major reasons for choice of alternative in Section IV above.

VI. Implementation, brief statements of actions to be taken in executing the decision, including personalities involved; enumerate these statements.

A complete example of this outline, applied to a specific decision problem, appears later in this chapter.

THE MODEL AND IMPLEMENTING PROCEDURES

In the use of the foregoing model, the decision-maker may want to consider a number of procedures that may make the model work more effectively for him. For example, in step 1—statements of relevant facts—the decision-maker must bear in mind that the number of relevant facts in any problematic situation depends upon the nature of the problem, the evidence available, and cost and time factors. Thus, in step 1 the decision-maker will need to make a preliminary factual analysis of the situation. Using his judgment and the fruits of his preliminary analysis, he should then attempt to get a preliminary notion of the problem. This may well lead to the need for additional facts. With the available facts, he may have a more refined definition of the problem, and he may be sent to gather more pertinent facts and to redefine the problem. This process will continue until the decision-maker feels that he has enough relevant facts and a sufficiently refined notion of the problem to state it in final form, bringing him to step 2—the problem statement.

With the relevant facts and the problem now stated, the decision-maker proceeds to step 3—the statements of alternatives. In this step, the individual should choose no less than three alternatives if possible. The reason for this is that we should think of our alternatives as lying along a continuum. If we assume that the best alternative is the unknown alternative X on the continuum, then what we are trying to do in step 3 is to get as close to X as possible. If we use at least three alternatives—namely A, B, and C—and select one for each of the two extremes on the continuum and one from a position near the center, and then select a D and an E, we may approximate what appears in Figure 9-1 below.

In listing the advantages and disadvantages for each alternative, we may find it a practical procedure to use a separate sheet of $8\frac{1}{2}'' \times 11''$ paper with a vertical line drawn down the middle for each alternative. On the left side we might list the advantages and on the right side the disadvantages. Or, if we have developed some facility with the columnar analysis sheets used by accountants and statisticians, we may find that a 12- to 30-column analysis sheet is quite useful. On a 30-column sheet, we can place the alternatives across the top horizontally with advantages and disadvantages listed under each alternative. Some people would like this approach; others would not. In any case, we have mentioned three possible approaches to the handling of alternatives: (1) the vertical listing as in the outline of our model; (2) the separate listing of an alternative on an $8\frac{1}{2}'' \times 11''$ sheet of paper; (3) the horizontal listing of many alternatives across the top of a columnar sheet with the related advantages and disadvantages listed vertically under each alternative (see Appendix A at the end of the chapter for this technique).

Whatever approach is followed, the decision-maker may find it quite necessary to revise the lists of advantages and disadvantages and the alternatives from time to time. Advantages and disadvantages need to be reexamined to permit elimination of duplications, to make sure that an advantage is actually an advantage, to see whether the decision-maker has inadvertently listed an advantage as a disadvantage or vice versa, to eliminate insignificant items, or to add items which he has thought about in the interim.

A	E	X	C	D	B

FIGURE 9-1. **An alternatives continuum.**

With the alternatives presented and their advantages and disadvantages evaluated, the decision-maker approaches step 4—the final decision. Although step 4 calls for a judgment, we must bear in mind that the decision-maker has used his judgment innumerable times already in deciding what facts are relevant, which problem to state for analysis, which alternatives to consider, and which advantages and disadvantages to investigate. After the decision-maker states his final decision, he then has a chance to verify his choice in step 5—final verification. Here he needs to make some brief summary statements of the major reasons for his choice in step 4. If after his verification his decision of step 4 still looks valid, he moves to step 6—implementation. In this final step of the model, the decision-maker asks himself about the practical probability of effective execution of the decision, especially considering the people involved in the organization. Some highly refined judgments may be necessary here to decide upon strategies to bring the decision-making process to a fruitful termination.

THE MODEL IN APPLICATION

We have now arrived at the point in our study which is probably most neglected by others, which involves a philosophical view of knowledge in general and of decision-making in particular. I think it is useless to know the principles of anything if one does not use them for their intended end. Perhaps the simplest way to state what I mean is in the proverb: The proof of the pudding is in the eating. In other words, the court of final appeal is not brilliant argumentation, or high-sounding abstract principles, or even precise logic or mathematics—it is the results in the real world. Therefore, in judging any system or model the acid test is, *does it work?* If a system or model does not work, it is of little value to the manager to know the fundamental truths of any science or art; a manager's knowledge needs to be put into practice, the development of cultural and prestigious aspects of the acquisition of knowledge notwithstanding. This pragmatic approach of the acid test—does it work?—is one way of looking at the real world, an outlook which, while in accord with scientists' attitudes, is not entirely in accord with attitudes that prevail outside the laboratories.[1] John Dewey has succinctly put it this way: "The true purpose of knowledge resides in the consequences of directed action."[2]

Let us now apply the model for decision-making to a real problem of an organization. We have learned that sensitivity to uncertainty depends upon the state of development of one's conceptual structure. A well developed conceptual framework is sensitive to challenging problems; a system of ideas that is not well constructed may fail to provide the necessary awareness of a problem and the accompanying uncertainty of what to do about it. In the case of The Chicago Metal Company,[3] Mr. Willis possesses a sufficiently sensitive conceptual structure because, prior to undertaking his new assignment, he anticipates a future situation that is characterized by changes and problems. His reflections regarding these changes and problems indicate that he is experiencing a feeling of uncertainty or doubt. It is precisely because Mr. Willis is aware of the existence of a problem that he feels uncertain. Stimulated by this feeling, Mr. Willis will begin to investigate the problematic situation. Let us now use the model as Mr. Willis would use it. Upon careful analysis, Mr. Willis discloses certain relevant facts and states them as follows:

THE CHICAGO METAL COMPANY

I. Statements of Relevant Facts:
  1. Decision-making power historically has been centralized in the home office.
  2. The plant manager now possesses much more discretionary power than in the past.

---

[1] Irwin D. F. Bross, *Design for Decision* (New York: Macmillan, 1953), p. 29.

[2] John Dewey, *The Quest for Certainty* (New York: Putnam, 1939).

[3] The Chicago Metal Company, a case problem which appears in Appendix B at the end of this chapter, should now be carefully studied and analyzed. The Chicago Metal Company is an actual business case with the name of the company and the names of all the individuals concerned disguised, and will be used to demonstrate the model for decision-making. Although The Chicago Metal Company is an industrial case, any kind of case could have been used—in public administration, hospital administration, educational administration, or military administration—for two reasons: (1) decision-making is essentially the same process anywhere; (2) a model should be generally applicable to be useful.

3. The organization has had a strong informal system of relationships in the past.
4. Profits are declining.
5. Competition is increasing.
6. Lower costs, reduced labor requirements, and improved uniformity of product quality are some of the goals top management is looking for from the experiment.
7. Management has taken the view that some form of relationship between the home office production staff and the plant manager should be retained, but only after a previous split on the issue and with the qualification that the final decision be made by Mr. Willis.
8. Mr Willis is charged with full responsibility for the success of the decentralized operation.
9. Top management has substantial confidence in Mr. Willis's ability.[4]

II. The Statement of the Problem:

By means of what organizational plan can Mr. Willis achieve effective control in the new operation so that the top management goals of reduced labor and other costs and improved uniformity of product quality may be realized?

III. Statements of Alternatives:

1. Use the proposed organizational structure (Exhibit II of Appendix B).
   1.1. *Advantages:*
      1.11. The proposed organizational structure has the support of top management.
      1.12. The plant manager will have increased technical knowledge available to him on a formal (staff) basis.
      1.13. The plant manager will be made aware of communications between home office and plant with respect

---

[4] As was indicated earlier, the disclosure of relevant facts is dominated to a great extent by the conceptual structure or value structure that the decision-maker brings to the facts. Since the statement of the problem significantly depends upon the factual analysis, it is in turn affected by one's system of ideas. Moreover, perception, emotion, values, habit or traditional behavior, physical condition, and the search for the road of least resistance affect the statement of the problem. Consequently, the reader should not be disturbed if he does not agree with my statement of the problem or the relevant facts. Whatever the relevant facts or the problem, the model is unchanged and still applies.

    to production control, engineering, methods, and quality control.

1.2. *Disadvantages:*

    1.21. The plant manager may receive advice from the assistant staff of the vice-president of production at the home office whether he wants it or not.

    1.22. The plant manager may act as a bottleneck in the communication process between the assistant staff of the vice-president of production and counterparts in the plant.

2. Use a plan of organizational structure with no divided authority (Exhibit II of Appendix B without the broken lines).

  2.1. *Advantages:*

    2.11. The plant manager could ask for advice when he wants it from the home office staff.

    2.12. The plant manager would perhaps operate on a more independent basis.

  2.2. *Disadvantages:*

    2.21. The plant manager might not seek technical advice when he should because of no formal relationship with the home office staff.

    2.22. Knowledge from the engineering, production control, and quality control departments and methods at the home-office would have to pass through the vice-president of production down to the plant manager, who in turn would have to pass the knowledge on to the men in charge of these departments in the plant.

    2.23. This organizational plan does not have the support of top management.

3. Use a plan of organizational structure with multiple line relationships (Exhibit II of Appendix B with the broken lines replaced by solid lines).

  3.1. *Advantages:*

    3.11. The plant manager will have technical knowledge available to him on a formal (line or functional) basis.

  3.2. *Disadvantages:*

    3.21. A selling job would be necessary to get the plan considered.

    3.22. The plant manager has too many superiors with line authority.

    3.23. The plant manager would act as a bottleneck in the communication process to the plant staff.

IV. Final Decision:

The plant manager should adopt Alternative 1—use the proposed organizational structure (Exhibit II of Appendix B).

V. Final Verification:

1. The major reason for the choice of Alternative 1 in step IV is that it has the support of top management, while the other two alternatives do not.
2. The relationship established in Alternative 1 between the plant manager and the assistant staff of the vice-president of production is a staff relationship of advice. Such a relationship gives the assistant staff of the vice-president of production no formal enforcement authority over the plant manager as does Alternative 3.
3. The disadvantages of Alternative 1 and the advantages of Alternative 2 and 3 seem less important than statements one and two above under V.

VI. Implementation:

1. The choice of Alternative 1 in Step IV unquestionably minimizes the problem of decision execution and acts as its own guide to implementation.
2. The vice-presidents of sales, procurement, production, and control already have virtually approved the decision, although originally they wanted all relationships between the home and plant manager cut off except the pure line relationship of the plant manager to the vice-president of production. This approval seems an automatic confirmation of Alternative 1. In this case, a mere communication of the decision would effect its execution.
3. The assistant staff of the vice-president of production wanted some kind of relationship with the plant manager. The staff got its wish. Again, a mere communication of the decision would effect its execution by this group.
4. The plant manager should decide the best way to communicate his decision to the two groups mentioned in 2 and 3 under VI. This could be done orally, by memorandum, or by a meeting. Since the members at a meeting gave the plant manager final authority to decide upon the organizational relationships, an expeditious method may well be by memorandum, thereby eliminating a meeting and reducing the decision to a written communication, with file copies as evidence that the plant manager actually made the communication.

The written communication might take the following form:

The Chicago Metal Company
(Memorandum)

TO: Vice-president of Production
FROM: George Willis
SUBJECT: Decision on Organizational Relationships in Decentral-
            ized Plant

After considerable reflection on several alternatives, it is my decision
to adopt the staff (advice) relationships between your assistant staff
and the plant manager as suggested by the committee. I will appreciate
any comments or thoughts you or your staff might have on the matter.

G. W.

This is the solution to the problem of The Chicago Metal
Company according to the model presented in this chapter. If the
solution appears lengthy to the reader, it should be kept in mind
that most major decisions do not have to be made at once, and
it is worth taking the time to increase the rational element in
decision-making. Yet the "suspension of judgment" which is essential to rational decision-making is difficult or impossible when
one is under pressure for "immediate action." If one's house is on
fire, he must act quickly and promptly—he cannot stop to consider the possible causes or to estimate the consequences of the
various ways of reacting. Similarly, when an organizational situation calls for an immediate decision, it is frequently better for
the executive to risk being wrong than to risk a delay. Nevertheless, it is amazing how one may speed up the decision-making
process after some practice.

A modified solution using a more rigorous model is presented
in Appendix C at the end of this chapter.

Appendix A. Compiling Alternatives

The column-ruled sheets used by accountants are easily
adapted to the listing of alternatives with their advantages and
disadvantages. This technique displays the statements of all alternatives for simultaneous examination.

The diagram below shows the first few column headings on a ruled sheet of this type. A 12-column sheet will display three alternatives, as follows:

	ALTERNATIVE 1		ALTERNATIVE 2	
	Advantages	Disadvantages	Advantages	Disadva

Appendix B. Case Description

THE CHICAGO METAL COMPANY

The Chicago Metal Company is a large metal manufacturing company with twelve plants scattered throughout various parts of the United States. Each plant employs from 500 to 1,000 persons.

The home office of the company is in downtown Chicago, commonly called the Loop. The chief executive officers of the company are located in the home office on State Street. These include the president, the executive vice-president, and the vice-presidents in charge of sales, production, procurement, finance, and control (accounting). The vice-president in charge of production has a manufacturing staff reporting to him, composed of the assistant vice-presidents of engineering, production control, quality control, and methods. Representatives of each of the home-office staff are located in each plant, and they are directly responsible to the plant manager as well as to their respective staff superiors in the home office (Exhibit I). Formally, this amounted to divided authority, but in practice the plant manager had little authority on an operating basis.

Since the company's founding in 1935 in a small shop on the far south side of Chicago, decision-making power has been centralized in the home office. In the past plant managers had no knowledge or notification of company plans until the production orders were on their desks. The personnel in the plant felt that operating decisions should be made as close to the operating activities as possible. Consequently, there was frequently friction between the home-office representatives and the plant personnel.

For several years the company has not been satisfied with profits, since competition seems to be getting keener. As an experiment, the home-office executive committee, which consists of all the executives in the Chicago office (Exhibit I), recently approved the operation of one of the company's modern plants on a somewhat decentralized basis. Top management has decided to test the claims of the plant personnel. Because new production methods would be employed, lower fabricating costs, reduced labor requirements, and improved uniformity of product quality are some of the goals top management anticipates from the new operation.

The man appointed to be manager of the new operation is Mr. George Willis. Mr. Willis has been with the company for six years in various capacities in engineering, production and quality control, and methods. Mr. Willis spent ten years as an accountant with a number of firms, holding the position of controller before coming to The Chicago Metal Company. While an accountant, Mr. Willis attended the University of Chicago and received a Master's degree in Business Administration in production management just before joining The Chicago Metal

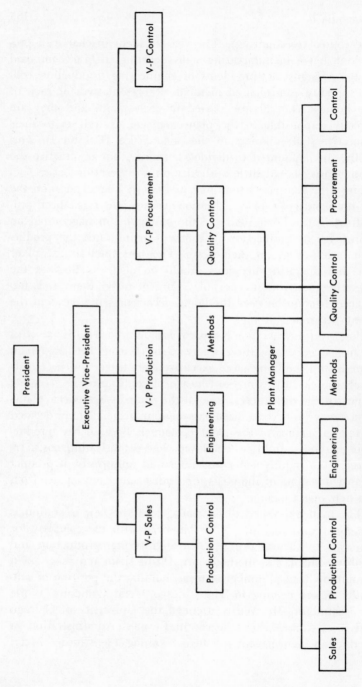

EXHIBIT I. The Chicago Metal Company—partial present organization.

Company. Anxious to get into production management, Mr. Willis has been a bundle of energy giving everything he has at The Chicago Metal Company. His demonstrated managerial ability, his reputation as a cost finder and a cost reducer, and the fact that he is a good man in human relations, gave him the necessary support for the appointment as manager of the pilot operation.

Although delighted with his new and challenging assignment, Mr. Willis is not unaware of the problems facing him. He realizes that a new experiment such as the one The Chicago Metal Company is undertaking after so many years under the central control of manufacturing operations will create major changes and problems. He will have a modern plant, new processes, new methods, new people, and new organizational relationships. Previously the plant manager dealt with the appropriate staff representation; if no satisfactory agreement was reached, he went to the vice-president of production. Under the new system the plant manager has much more discretionary power and may deal directly with the vice-president of production.

At the final meeting of the home-office executive committee concerning organization, a difference of opinion developed. The vice-presidents of sales, procurement, production, and control wished to have all relationships between the home office and the plant manager cut off except for the pure line relationship of the plant manager to the vice-president of production. However, the assistant staff of the vice-president of production at the home office (engineering, production control, quality control, and methods) felt that some relationship between the staff and the plant manager should be retained (Exhibit II). Because the home-office staff of the vice-president of production felt so strongly about retaining some form of direct hierarchical relationship with the new plant manager, and since they were all production people, the remaining members of the executive committee decided after considerable discussion to go along with them. However, the members did so only on the condition that Mr. Willis be given final authority to decide upon the organizational relationships, since he will be responsible for the success of the decentralization experiment. This was agreed to and the meeting adjourned.

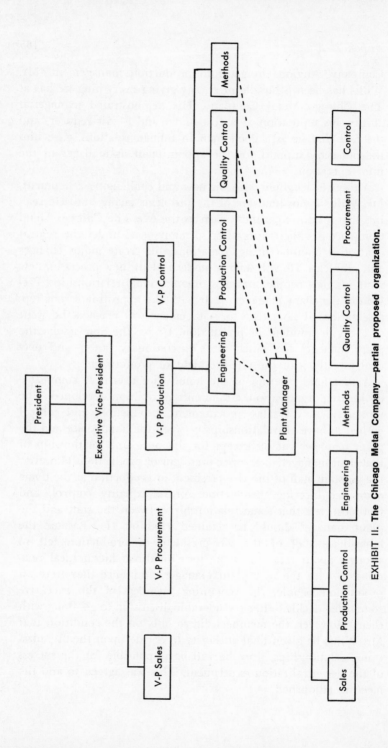

EXHIBIT II. The Chicago Metal Company—partial proposed organization.

Appendix C. Some Notes on the Application of the Deductive Method

For those who are familiar with the deductive method or who wish to become familiar with it,[5] the following additional step may be added to the model presented in this chapter. Deductive treatment of an alternative involves syllogistic reasoning. Accordingly, Mr. Willis may formally commence his logical reasoning process by setting up the following hypothetical syllogism:

Either the proposed organizational structure will yield control, or a plan of organizational structure with no divided authority will yield control.

But the proposed organizational structure will yield control (because it has the support of top management).

Therefore, a plan of organizational structure without divided authority will not yield control.

This argument is a valid hypothetical disjunctive syllogism. It may be employed to eliminate suggested solutions to problems. In this case, Mr. Willis has used it to negate his suggested alternative 2. The disjunctive syllogism similarly may be used to eliminate any third alternative as follows:

Either the proposed organizational structure will yield control or any other plan of organizational structure will yield control.

But the proposed organizational structure will yield control (because it has the support of top management).

Therefore, any other plan of organizational structure will not yield control.

The elimination of alternatives 2 and 3 does not, however, establish the truth of alternative one. Alternative one must be formally established. Therefore, Mr. Willis must reason further. He may then develop the following hypothetical syllogism with respect to his alternative one:

If the proposed organizational structure has the support of top management, it will yield control.

[5] See R. W. Morell, *Managerial Decision-Making* (Milwaukee: Bruce, 1960), for a complete discussion of this method.

But the proposed organizational structure has the support of top management.
Therefore, the proposed organizational structure will yield control.

This is a valid hypothetical conditional syllogism. It formally establishes the validity of alternative one.

From the foregoing analysis, Mr. Willis may decide that he should adopt alternative one. He should realize, however, that although his process of logical reasoning has established the validity of alternative one, the truth of his conclusions depends upon the truth of his premises. Unfortunately, logic is no protection against error in the formulation of the premises.

The administrator is primarily interested in the truth of his decision rather than in its validity. To establish the truth of his decision to adopt alternative 1, Mr. Willis must further analyze the decision. The second (minor) premise of the above conditional syllogism can be established by observation of the relevant facts of the situation, and induction. The first (major) premise, however, is not so easily verified. Here the categorical syllogism can play a vital role. For example, Mr. Willis could set up the following categorical syllogisms:

Final authority rests with top management.
Efficient organizational structures are based upon final authority.
Therefore, efficient organizational structures rest with top management.

Then,

The support of top management will yield control.
The proposed organizational structure has the support of top management.
Therefore, the proposed organizational structure will yield control.

These categorical syllogisms are valid logical forms of the AAA and AII variety respectively. The major premises in the above categorical syllogisms are in the nature of fundamental truths or principles. Mr. Willis, being a prudent man, will avail himself of all the principles of administration, economics, and other relevant sciences which he has at his command before coming to his final decision. Accordingly, the first and fourth premises in the above categorical syllogisms will be statements of what Mr. Willis believes to be sound and true principles. If they are not, then his search for truth will reap no harvest this time. We hope that he will adjust his concepts in the future as he discovers that they are not true. On the other hand, if the first and fourth premises are true (and Mr. Willis has to go on the assumption that they are), then the conclusion of the conditional syllogism is not only valid but is also true. Consequently, Mr. Willis should adopt alternative one.

Discussion Questions

1. Why is it important to apply what we know?
2. What is the most difficult—learning principles or application of principles? Why?
3. Explain the statement that "decision-making is essentially the same process anywhere."
4. What does the statement of the problem depend upon?
5. What is a problem? What is a fact?
6. What are *relevant* facts?
7. Why was it necessary to demonstrate the solution of a problem in this chapter?
8. Of what use is a model for managers?
9. What kind of a model is the one presented in this chapter?
10. Is "model building" a "panacea"? Why or why not?
11. What are some alternatives to the use of a model in decision-making?
12. What qualities may the use of a model develop in the decision-maker?
13. Why is it important to write things down in the use of models?
14. Of what value is an alternative's continuum?
15. What would be some of the criticisms of the pragmatic test—does it work?

16. Do most scientists support the pragmatic approach? Why or why not?
17. Would the layman support the pragmatic approach? Explain.
18. "The true purpose of knowledge resides in the consequences of directed action." Discuss.
19. "A model to be useful should be generally useful." True or false? Explain.
20. The goal of methodical attempts in decision-making such as the use of logic and/or models should be to increase rationality in decision-making. True or false? Explain.

References

Bross, Irwin D., *Design for Decision* (New York: Macmillan, 1953), Chapter 10.

Bryson, Lyman, "Notes on Theory of Advice," *Political Science Quarterly*, LXVI, No. 3 (September, 1951), 321-339.

Calhoun, S. Reed, and Paul E. Green, "Simulation—Versatile Aid to Decision-Making," *Advanced Management*, Vol. 23, (April, 1958), 11-16.

Dale, Ernest, "New Perspectives in Managerial Decision-Making," *Journal of Business*, XXVI (January, 1953), 1-8.

Dennison, Henry S., "Decision-Making at the Top Executive Level," *Papers and Proceedings of the Sixty-Third Annual Meeting of the American Economic Association*, Chicago, December 27 to December 30, 1950, XLI, No. 2 (AEA) (1951), 98-105.

Katona, George, and J. M. Morgan, "The Quantitative Study of Factors Determining Business Decisions," *Quarterly Journal of Economics*, LXVI, No. 1 (February, 1952), 67-90.

Lindsay, Franklin A., *New Technique for Management Decision-Making* (New York: McGraw-Hill, 1958), Parts 2, 3.

McCamy, Jones L., "Analysis of the Process of Decision-Making," *Public Administrative Review*, VII, No. 1 (Winter, 1947), 41-48.

McDonald, John, "How Businessmen Make Decisions," *Fortune*, LII, No. 2 (August, 1955) 84-87, 120, 132, 137.

McDonald, John, and Frank Ricciardi, "The Business Decision Game," *Fortune,* LVII, No. 3 (March, 1958), 140-142, 208.

Morell, R. W., *Managerial Decision-Making* (Milwaukee: Bruce, 1960), Chapters 3-9.

Morell, R. W., "Managerial Decision-Making—A Challenge," *Marquette Business Review,* I, No. 3 (December, 1957), 1-6.

Morell, R. W., "What is a Decision"? *Hospital Progress,* Vol. 39, No. 2 (February, 1958), 74, 95.

Schnelle, K. E., *Case Analysis and Business Problem Solving* (New York: McGraw-Hill, 1967), Chapters 3-11.

Simon, H. A., "Decision-Making and Administrative Organization," *Public Administration Review,* IV, No. 1 (Winter, 1944), 16-30.

Sufbik, Forest D., "Executive Decisions at the Top Level," *Papers and Proceedings of the Sixty-Third Annual Meeting of the American Economic Association,* Chicago, December 27 to December 30, 1950, XLI, No. 2 (AEA) (1951), 88-92.

Chapter 10

Conclusions

My idea of an agreeable person is a person
who agrees with me.—BENJAMIN DISRAELI

In the introduction to this book management was defined as
that activity which consists of deciding upon the goals of an organization and of deciding upon the means and functions by
which the goals are to be reached. I also stated that the philosophy of management is concerned with what management ought
to do rather than with what management is actually doing, with
a view to making judgments and/or inferences about the activities
constituting management. This is the purpose of this chapter—
to generalize, not to summarize. Of course, a person must be
cautious in making generalizations or inferences. Moreover, the
history of man and the history of management warns us not to
expect easy and proximate fulfillment of moral aspirations
and/or justification of management activities. Nevertheless, I feel
compelled at this point to make some inferences regardless of the
consequences. For what would one's philosophy of management
be if he did not finally come to some definitive, critical statements
about management, especially when such statements follow analysis? Yet these are just one man's thoughts about management.

First, many organizations today still do not have a clear-cut
hierarchy of goals precisely written out. I think this is unfortunate, because I find it difficult to accept the notion of striving
for goals that are not clearly formulated in the mind as well as
in writing. It is inefficient to expend effort in the area of means
when the goals have not been meticulously spelled out. For when
the goals are not precisely stated, there is no clear way to reach
them. Specifically, the employment goal and the return-to-labor
goal need to be more fully appreciated by more managers if government intervention is to be minimized in the future.

192

Second, many managers' concept of the environment of organizations is much too narrow and needs to be broadened, primarily through exposure to the social and behavioral sciences, philosophy, law, quantitative and computer aspects of management, and other relevant disciplines. For some, independent study may be a suitable approach; for others, outside help may be necessary, perhaps from a consultant with or without development programs. Finally, for those still in school—the leaders of the future—the necessary background should be acquired during their formal education.

Third, the nature of management, including what management actually is, needs to be more clearly understood by many administrators. The notion that one is born with managerial knowledge is primitive in contemporary Western society. It is not accidental that since World War II many older countries of Western Europe have looked to the United States for leadership in managerial knowledge. The idea that a man is born with leadership traits or talents is of course still valid, but using that talent is another matter. One cannot effectively practice what one does not know; and one only knows an art or science through study and experience. For example, a medical student would not practice medicine on a patient until he has studied anatomy and physiology. A man whose title includes or implies the word "manager" is not necessarily a manager, for to be one he must know what management is, how to practice it, and he must actually practice it. Unfortunately, knowledge of management is often assumed, with the result that many people with high administrative and executive positions hold them because of accident, error, friendship, or politics rather than because of their knowledge of management.

Fourth, I believe that choice is at the heart of the administrative process. If one cannot make good decisions most of the time, he cannot be a good manager no matter what other qualities he may have. The manager who makes decisions by hunch, impulse, chance, or on some other hit-or-miss basis is out-of-date and is using untrustworthy methods. A person does anything better if he knows what he is doing, why he is doing it, and how to do it. Thus, by tackling the decision-making process rationally and by deliberately putting it to work for him, the manager will augment his other talents as a decision-maker. While making decisions, he should also become aware of factors such as perception, emotion, values, habits, groups, culture, and physical condition. Being conscious of these subjective factors can be of great value in raising the rational level of one's decision-making behavior. Moreover, a manager should not expect his decisions to be any better than the process he used to arrive at them. Sloppy methods will almost always yield sloppy decisions, while a methodical approach to decision-making will undoubtedly yield more valid and true decisions. We can only imagine the higher standard of living that we might have if managers made better decisions. Greater efficiency, lower costs, increased quality, and reduced prices are some of the advantages of replacing rule-of-thumb by rule-of-head —replacing the guess by the well thought-out decision.

Finally, although most organizations cannot be expected to function as a family, a church, a clinic, or a charitable institution, nevertheless human justice and equity cannot be ignored in the long run without damage to the organization. Problems arise in organizations in which people's feelings are not only ignored by some administrators but are deliberately or inadvertently hurt. In either case, people suffer great injustices that cannot be recovered by policies and for which there seems to be little or no redress. This is unfortunate for most individuals who must work for a living because their subordinate position usually precludes their taking remedial action. Because of this, we must look to the manager who conveys justice and equity in all his decisions and actions in such a way that his subordinates know that righteousness prevails. When more managers accept and practice justice rather than caprice, favoritism, and punishment, going to work for many people will become a pleasurable experience rather than a painful one, with a consequent concern with living rather than with merely making a living. Thus, the world will be a better place in which to work and live.

Index